# THE POWER OF
# NOT YET

*Living a Life of Endless Possibilities*

Donna Pisani

To my Mom and Dad – thanks for always believing in me and being the most incredible example of strength, love and encouragement *all* of my life.

To the love of my life, Dennis. Thank you for *always* and forever being my biggest cheerleader and seeing the leader in me even when I didn't. Love you forever.

To Bethany, Jessica, Gabs, and Evan, you have been and always will be the joy of my heart. This book is for you. May you always know how much God is for you and that Dad and I are cheering you on. May you live to your fullest potential as you discover your own *Gloria* and all that God made possible *in you.*

Most of all to God. You are magnificent in every way., especially your unceasing, unlimited love healing my heart and using the broken pieces of my life to inspire others. Thank you for taking a scared teenager on the journey of a lifetime. I am forever grateful.

And to you, dear reader, who is feeling a bit stuck and are tired of hearing *not yet.* This is for you; may you awaken to your unique purpose, expose the fears, and go change the world.

# Table of Contents

# Introduction

Imagine what it feels like to hit only green lights on your morning commute. Or what an obstacle-free life would look like, one in which every dream that seamlessly formulates in your mind becomes reality.

Oh the bliss of *that* life!

Every day and from every angle you are promised success if you just follow this three-step plan or that twelve-step program. Perfectly finished and tied up with a bow, and off you ride into the sunset without a care in the world. You safely and easily arrive at your destination.

Easy breezy perfection, right?

I recently found myself sitting on a beach in paradise, sipping my tropical drink, and realizing at that moment my life was pretty close to perfection. Teasing thoughts flooded my mind, tempting me to just stay right where I was and skip out on all the responsibilities waiting for me back home. If only I could live here, I thought to myself.

But the reality is I don't.

And believe it or not, I have found that life isn't always as dreamy as sipping drinks in paradise. The reality is sometimes life is just hard.

Really hard.

Watching your dream come to pass often involves overcoming various obstacles, the threat of resistance keeping you stalled mid-process.

Resistance.

I think you know what I'm talking about. And the more resistance you face, the more you begin to feel stuck. Perhaps a dull restlessness that began as a whisper has become a roar you can no longer ignore.

The feeling of waiting, the moments when we hear *not yet* can often feel like an internment in a prison camp in which we long to escape and get on with life. Every passing moment, day, and year appears as if nothing is moving.

Often paralyzed with the fear of failure, you feel stuck.

## THE FAMILY CIRCUS

The inspiration to take a road trip with four kids always involved a bit of insanity and grasping at the hope that we were not failure parents. Often our road trips felt like a reality TV show, and I hoped to God no one could hear the dialogue taking place among the six of us.

The expectation of a glorious family time was often stymied by the intricacies of navigating the different personalities of our amazing kids. How did God see fit in His infinite wisdom to give us not one but four choleric/leader children, all of whom felt their calling was to lead the "Pisani Family Circus" road trip? While there were no elephants in our circus there was plenty of hilarity and tension. Aside from trying to establish strong battle boundary lines before taking off, we always had to double our travel time. As every good parent knows, tiny bladders never, ever have to use the bathroom at the same time. And those little guys are usually triggered ten minutes and five seconds after the previous bathroom stop, which would equal 147 stops in a six-hour trip.

All the while, the "melodious" sound on repeat from the back seat—and always in unison by all four—was the echo heard every five minutes:

"Are we there yet?"

Young minds don't understand time. And even though our immediate response was, "Not yet," laced with threats of time out if we heard the question one more time, it didn't stop the squirming with anticipation in the back seat of reaching the destination.

What about you?

Quite possibly, you've also been squirming through life, echoes of *Are we there yet* on repeat in your own head.

The middle is the hardest place to exist because we can't write on the calendar the exact date and time the season is over, or when that everlasting feeling of being stuck in the Not Yet Zone will go away. Our fears try to hold us back and define us, but we must remember fear is *loud* liar:

"You should be further along now than you are."

"You must have failed or you wouldn't be stuck here."

"You're going to have to deal with these issues forever."

"You don't have what it takes to get unstuck."

"You are destined to always be a "two" in a number one world."

"You're not smart enough, and not gifted enough."

"You will never get off the runway and fly how you were created to."

Yet all you *really* want to do is fly.

I know exactly how you feel. I have been there: exhausted because I allowed myself to remain stuck because of the circumstances around me, feeling there was something simple I was missing that allowed others to take off.

I've believed God could turn things around, but I had no idea how this would happen. I experienced the debilitating, immobilizing pain of living years imprisoned by insecurity, comparison, and the crippling mindset that I would always be second.

For years I was silenced by insecurity; the fear had a chokehold on my confidence and destiny. I was dressed in the shame of the sexual abuse I experienced as a child, which kept the authentic me from being known. But I've discovered a few powerful concepts that set me free, and I believe if you too can grasp these they will set you free as well.

Simply put, having the right perspective here in the middle is golden, because if we aren't careful with our thoughts and beliefs, we can define ourselves by the resistance, and the God-given potential and purpose remain hidden.

What if I were to tell you that place of feeling stuck is not defined by failure, but that the Not Yet Zone is actually a set up for a life of *endless possibilities*? That this place of waiting actually makes us stronger, smarter, and prepares us to experience the incredible potential God has woven into our purpose? The truth is, the place of waiting is not diminishing you; it's building you!

You are brilliant. God has hardwired into you a magnificent purpose. You are brimming with potential to not only have a happy life, but to help others do the same. You are a world changer; you are significant, and we all need what you bring to the table.

Yes, *you*.

My hope is as you read this book, you will discover you don't have to feel stuck any longer. I share four things that have helped me overcome fear, stop hustling for acceptance, and walk boldly in the courage to see the turnaround God has already written into my own story.

We have all been entrusted by God with powerful stories that give each of us authority to lead ourselves well, and I'm going to help you discover the simplicity of these in each section of the book.

We've been entrusted with Choice; I will teach you how to flip the switch and expose the fears you've been soothing for far too long.

We've been entrusted with the Not Yet Zone; I will show you small steps that will significantly impact you to become smarter and stronger while you wait in the process.

We've been entrusted with Brave; I will show you how God has already written all over your story that you win and you will discover how to see and say it. Understanding God's purpose is always bigger than what you think or even imagine and His desire to see you fulfill it is even greater than your longing for it!

We've been entrusted with leadership I will show you how to lead yourself well and to discover the purpose God has placed in you, removing the confusion of knowing how to start.

The principles in this book changed my life over the past thirty-five years, and I know they will change yours too. I have seen so many people set free from the fear that bellows in the hidden places. I love watching the transformation that consistently happens.

I will show you how what you think about your season is more important than the season around you actually changing.

Haven't you been waiting on the runway long enough? Tired of living small? Feel called to greatness?

It's your time, friend, right here in the middle. You've been wired to change the world; my hope is that you uncover your potential and see how to overcome once and for all the fear that is suffocating the life out of you and begin living a life of *endless possibilities*.

This is your invitation to come along this journey with me; I believe you'll find yourself in this story just like I did.

I believe in you. And so does God; in fact, all of heaven is cheering you on!

This is *your* time.

Donna xoxo

# PART I

# ENTRUSTED WITH CHOICE

*She never seemed shattered; to me, she was a breathtaking mosaic of the battles she won.*

— Matt Baker —

# 1

# Like Clockwork

I would awaken to her tiny, sweet face staring at me, close enough that I could feel her panicked breath on my cheek. Then, like a record on repeat, I would hear that same little human voice begin to spill out the terrors of the night, the things she imagined in the dark corners of her room.

Of course I knew there were no one-eyed, hairy monsters (thank you very much, Monsters, Inc.) lurking under her bed or evil creatures sneaking around in her closet. But because it was three o'clock in the morning and I was in the midst of sheer exhaustion from a very full life—four kids and a church to pastor—I would grab her tiny body, wrap my reassuring mama arms around her, and pull her into bed with me. Both of us were quickly engulfed in the warmth of blankets and pillows, as I tenderly prayed and quieted her fears until she dropped off to sleep.

This continued for weeks, until one night I realized all I was doing for this little one was *soothing* her fears, rather than showing her how to break this nightly routine of terror. All I had to do was remind her that she had a light switch in her room; that as tiny as she was, she had the power to switch the light on all by herself to expose the fear and silence her roaring imagination.

What about you?

How often does fear, the disappointment of an unmet expectation, or an out of control imagination scream at you, making you forget you have the power to turn on the light and expose it? God has an extraordinary plan for your life. Every single one of His promises has the power to silence any fear or disappointment in your life. It's time to stop soothing your fear and turn on the light.

What do you need to bring out of the darkness? Having that conversation? Starting a business? Writing a book? Stepping out of your comfort zone in order to chase a dream that has been stirring around in your soul and keeping you awake at night?

Perhaps this is your first time looking at the fear head on. Or maybe, like most of us, this is not your first time to the rodeo. You are well aware of the fear that is keeping you lassoed, locked down, held back, muffled, and gagged, with your stomach tangled in knots the size of Texas.

Fist pump.

You get the picture. If you're nodding your head right now and thinking, that's totally me, then you've picked up the right book.

You see yourself, bold and brave. Even kindergarteners know their aspirations to become President or to change the world. But somewhere in the wait, between five-year-old you and adult you, life happened. Between the joys of life and the stretching difficulties, you might have begun to feel as though the potential wasn't as great as you thought. This sobering realization has the capability and potential to paralyze you with fear and rob you of a bright future.

And so you settled into the dark room—comfortably uncomfortable—waiting for someone to turn the light on for you.

But it's time to turn your own light on, dear one.

"Woman in Rags, Garbage, Revealed as Heiress," read the headline of the San Francisco Chronicle concerning a lady known as "Garbage Mary" who was picked up by the authorities in a shopping mall in Delray Beach, Florida. She appeared to be just another seemingly homeless person whose mind had faded. Neighbors told stories of her scrounging through garbage cans for food, which she hoarded in her car and her two-bedroom apartment. There were mounds of garbage filling her small apartment's refrigerator, stove, sink, cabinets, and bathtub.

Police finally identified her as the daughter of a well-to-do lawyer and bank director from Illinois who had died several years earlier. In addition to the garbage, police found Mobil Oil stock, documents indicating ownership of oil fields in Kansas, stock certificates from firms such as U.S. Steel, Uniroyal, and Squibb, along with passports for eight large bank accounts. Garbage Mary was a millionaire who lived as a derelict. She had untold wealth at her disposal, and yet she scrounged through garbage cans rather than claim the resources that were rightly hers.[1]

What about you, friend?

Do you scrounge through the garbage rather than claim the inheritance that awaits you? There's a wealth of potential with far greater value than Garbage Mary's total net worth at your disposal. Fear keeps that potential hidden, dormant, and locked up as tight as Fort Knox.

Perhaps tucked into that fear of turning on the light is the belief it will also expose the "garbage" you'd rather keep covered up, the broken, the bruised, and the cracks of imperfection that have left you feeling disqualified from harnessing your God given gifts. Surely God can't use me in this condition, you think. And so you keep it pushed back into the dark corners of your life where it feels more safe and less exposed.

But guess what; no one is perfect. And as much as I hate to admit it, this includes me. Not even close.

It's only nine o'clock in the morning and I could already give you a list of my top twenty imperfect moments since I got out of bed. Between pouring OJ in my coffee because my exhausted eyes are only half open, to finding myself in an uncontrolled, irritated state because of the debris scattered around the house in the wake of my four kids. By the time I sit down to have a quiet moment to read my Bible, I am already feeling the shadow of defeat hovering over me. And that's just the beginning! On another day remind me to tell you about the time I fell off the platform I was speaking on, or the time I handed a male Senator a sanitary pad instead of the business card he asked for, and any number of other embarrassing moments.

Raging insecurities and lies tell me that my less-than-perfect past or present day failures disqualify me from being used, and that while I might have God-given potential I should wait until after I get it together to make a move. But the promise to get it all together by tomorrow always seems just beyond my reach.

For centuries it seems that cemeteries have contained the richest caches of unused potential. Dreamers, history makers, inventors, scientists, world changers, global leaders, and missionaries—they're all laid to rest with unused potential, because even the greatest among us were crippled by fear. Who knows how the world would have benefited by what now lies unused.

The impetus behind the success of Apple was the incredible potential in Steve Jobs, whose creative genius changed the way we do life. Somewhere along the line he turned the light on to expose the fear of failure. He left Apple at age thirty, devastated after being unceremoniously removed from the company he started, only to return years later to lead the company to becoming one of the most profitable businesses in the world. He understood that failure was a jumping point to success. He often said, "Being the richest man in the cemetery doesn't matter to me; going to bed at night saying we've done something wonderful, that's what matters to me."[2]

He turned the light on.

But because of the lie, we are all conditioned to believe perfection is required to reach our potential. What you may not realize is that those scars of imperfection aren't a sideline to your story; they *are* your story. Each chapter is made beautiful by a God who loves you and will use you, not in spite of your imperfections but because of them.

Perhaps turning the light on means becoming vulnerable. Like, oops-my-shirt-is-on-backward-it's-a-bad-hair-day vulnerable. Be willing to look at yourself as the spotlight reveals your imperfections and persistent failure. Sounds crazy, right? Not really; every one of those cracks and crevices is costly and a means of celebration that you showed up. Hey, that *is* something to celebrate; in fact, *you* are something to celebrate! You are so filled with incredible gifts—more than you can imagine—hard wired into who you are, only made more rich by the experiences in your life.

What if Michael Jordan—winner of six NBA championships—had listened to his high school basketball coach and given up when he was cut from the team? Failure only inspired him to work harder. He said, "I have failed over and over again in my life but that is why I succeeded."[3]

Or Walt Disney, when he was fired from his first newspaper job because he was "lacking imagination and had no original ideas"? His first animation company went bankrupt, but he didn't sit in the dark waiting for someone else to flip the switch; he founded Walt Disney Company, which had over $40 billion in revenue in 2013.[4]

Or what about the Beatles? They were rejected by Decca Recording, who said they didn't like their sound and they had no future in show business. Their first single went on to sell more copies than any other song in the UK, making history and changing the course of music forever.[5]

A young Oprah Winfrey was demoted from her job as a news anchor because she was told she wasn't fit for television, but we all know she has become one of the most recognized faces in our generation. Oprah says, "Whatever you fear the most has no power; your fear of it is what has power, and once you face that truth, it will really set you free."[6]

Even the future of one of the most brilliant minds, Albert Einstein, was challenged from a young age. He couldn't even speak until he was four years old; his teacher said he would never amount to much. Now he is considered the most influential physicist of the twentieth century. He not only developed the theory of relativity but went on to win a Nobel Peace Prize.[7]

Jack Canfield was rejected 144 times before he found a publisher for his book, Chicken Soup for the Soul. When Jack told his publisher he wanted to sell one and a half million books in the first eighteen months, his publisher laughed and said he would be lucky if he could sell even twenty thousand copies. The first book sold more than eight million copies in America and ten million copies around the world. His advice? "The reality is that you just have to say 'I am more committed to my vision than I'm committed to doubt and fear,' then just go for it."[8]

Addressing Harvard University's commencement ceremony in 2008, J. K. Rowling spoke about failure: "You might never fail on the scale I did, but it is impossible to live without failing at something, unless you live so cautiously that you might as well not have lived at all—in which case, you fail by default." When Rowling wrote her first Harry Potter book, she was divorced, bankrupt, and on welfare. After a dozen rejections, one publisher finally agreed to publish her manuscript, but with the expectation that Rowling get a job because there's no money in children's books. She's now the first female fiction novelist billionaire.[9]

The lesson? Do not let your fears determine your destiny! Every one of these legends have something in common with you and I, they were imperfect and had failed—*and* were full of unlimited potential and endless possibilities.

The only difference is they stopped soothing their fears and turned on the light to expose them. They all obtained their greatest successes just a few steps beyond their greatest failure.

And so can you.

Perhaps taking that one step beyond failure is a key part of not letting your fears determine your destiny. My hope is that this book fans into flame what is already simmering as embers in your soul. So even if it feels like just smoldering ashes right now, I want you to know that if you look a little closer you'll see a flickering light.

# 2

# You are More than Enough

*Fear is an idea – debilitating, experience crushing, success-stalling inhibitor inflicted only by yourself.*

— Stephanie, Barista —

Waiting for the best cappuccino in DC is well worth it. I have been known to drive great distances for great coffee. But added to the tantalizing delight the caffeine gives me, overhearing, the barista behind the bar, talk about why she had waited so long to apply to college, was a powerful reminder of the disconnect that fear brings to the purpose God gives. She had just applied and felt an overwhelming sense of joy as she took one step forward toward unleashing her potential.

*One step.*

I so want you to fulfill your greatest potential, find your calling, and then summon the courage to live it; your contribution to humanity is more significant than you know.

My iPhone has so much potential. It's actually a small computer in my hand. Not only can I find a friend's phone number, but I can also find information about anything, from the population of the Congo, to current news, driving directions, and recommendations for the best restaurant in town. And this is all without the help of Siri, my virtual assistant—there isn't anything she can't answer! But even with all the features I do know how to use, I've barely tapped into the capabilities of my smart phone.

It was years before I stumbled on some of the genius things Siri can do. What a lifesaver to discover that while driving all I have to do is ask Siri for directions, or to open my iTunes to my favorite playlist. And realizing the simple time-saving fact that I could drop a pin on the map to find my car in a lot three hours after parking was a life changer! Anyone of you so busy in life that you forget where you parked your car at the mall?

My phone's potential is not diminished whether I use it or not. All the capabilities are still there. The same goes for your potential; it's not diminished whether you use it or not.

But untapped potential has a direct impact on your future.

Your past doesn't determine your potential; whether anyone notices you or not doesn't determine your potential; and neither does any unfair treatment, injustice, or disappointment you encounter. God, your Creator, determines your potential. He's hardwired it into you.

In fact, He said He knew us before He formed us in our mothers' wombs. Before we were born He set us apart.[10] Not one detail has escaped His love: He knows every hair on your head; He's numbered them, and He tells us to not be afraid because we are more valuable to Him than anything.[11]

If I don't take the time to charge my phone, normal daily usage tends to drain the battery. You may not realize it, but if you don't pay attention to the fear that is speaking to you, it will begin to drain your image of what is possible in your life. Everyday life tends to do that, but intentional connection to the right power source is essential to quelling the fear and living out your potential.

You were planted right where you are, right now, in this specific location and specific time, to produce a particular fruit. You have a unique assignment. You could have been born in another era: the Dark Ages, the French Revolution, or in the pioneer days. But God chose your life for now. (Is anyone else grateful that God waited until there was indoor plumbing to put you on the planet?)

You could have had different parents, but God knew no matter how good or bad they were, it was His plan for you to have the parents you had because you required the DNA that could only come from them.

You may have picked another face or body type, (shout out to all my fellow pear shapes!). Maybe you would have preferred a different personality type too, whether strong and outgoing, or quiet and subdued. Whether you're the life of the party, the take charge, let-me tell-you-what-to-do, or the creative thinker, if it were up to you, you might have tweaked things slightly.

But God had something in mind designed perfectly for you.

He talked you into existence. God is an architect and designer: He drew you up before you were born and planted you in the here and now, for this very moment.

You should know you have an enemy who wants you to despise where you've been.[12] God has a way of planting His best seed in His best soil. You may still despise it. I did for too many years of my life. It was that whole greener grass complex. At some point I had to stop listening to the lies and realize God planned it this way, and His strength is made perfect in our weakness.

You may have spent so much of your life waiting for the next season. When I was thirteen I couldn't wait to be sixteen so I could get my drivers license; I thought that's when I would really start living. But once I turned sixteen, I dreamed of going to college and getting out from under my parents control; I believed *then* life would be perfect. Once in college, I thought that as soon as I got married my life would be perfect. And once I was married, I couldn't wait to have kids. I lived in the consistent cycle of *if only this then....* I was certain the grass was greener on the other side.

There really is something called Greener Grass Syndrome.[13] People who suffer from it are afraid to live fully in this present moment, constantly waiting for a better next moment. But guess what! The grass is green right where you are; you just have to water it by being present! And while it feels like you're stuck waiting for another season, I believe there is gold to mine right where you are. And just like a GPS requires your current location to get you to where you're headed, you have to take account of where you are now.

# 3

# They Don't get the Last Say

Your value, your gifts, and your strengths have all been placed within you by God Himself. Honestly, it doesn't matter what anyone has spoken over you, or what your past failures, hurts, shame, condemnation or experiences have shouted at you. What God speaks over you is the final word.

The *final word*. (Just in case you missed that the first time.)

Any thought in you that doesn't inspire hope is under the influence of a lie.

And when we dwell on those thoughts that God isn't speaking or thinking, it creates a downward spiral that feels as difficult to get out of as if we are scaling Mount Everest.

You may have heard it said before that there is nothing new under the sun. The pattern of lies that mark us isn't new, nor are you and I the only ones to ever have dealt with them. Isn't there something weirdly comforting when you hear that someone else is dealing with the same things you are? I'm not sure if it's misery loving company or just knowing I am not alone in my struggle that brings the most comfort! It's been said, "There's no pain on earth that doesn't crave a benevolent witness."[14]

The same lies that have been used to distract and isolate humans since the garden of Eden still echo today. In the garden, after Adam and Eve tasted the forbidden fruit from the one tree God asked them not to— the tree of knowledge of good and evil, they hid weighted down with the shame of their sin.[15]

It was in this moment when God asked them, "Where are you?" We all know when God asks this question, it's not because He's lost you, but because He wants you to take an account of where you are, because perhaps you have become lost yourself.

As a child I often pictured the setting of this story, a lush garden filled with the most delightful greenery and woven with the full spectrum of color and every type of flower and fruit. In my mind it was *easy* to hide here.

How amazing is God's response to them? *"Adam, who told you, you were naked?* In no way was God disregarding their sin or disobedience, the fact that Adam and Eve recognized their sin was monumental, but He knew this was a defining moment in His relationship with them and for us. I don't believe it was a condemning criticism but a reality check given in love and strength. I believe God knew this one thing would be the greatest struggle all of humanity would wrestle with.

Identity.

It always has been and always will be about identity. Surely Adam and Eve had disobeyed God, but they were cowering and hiding in shame from the One who had the solution for their sin and failure. The conviction they felt because they disobeyed came from God, the urgency to *hide* their sin from God was the lies of shame and condemnation speaking.

When we find ourselves hiding *from* God in the shame of our brokenness, instead of running *to* Him; I believe God speaks the same thing to us... "Who told you, you were naked?" "Who told you there was something so wrong with you, you felt you had to hide from me? Come to me and we can work on this together."

As I look over my life, I reflect on how often I have seen my own "naked" brokenness, and instead of running *to* a loving God I've hidden in the dark hoping to get it together before I approach Him. Far too often we define ourselves by the sin and brokenness instead of the unlimited redemptive grace of a loving Father through the ultimate sacrifice of Christ over two thousand years ago. It not only affects the relationship God desires with us, it makes us feel we are not worthy of the purpose God has uniquely designed in us. You are not what your past failures and current imperfections say you are, you are a child of God, His masterpiece, redeemed and liberated from hiding in the dark.

And the battle rages on. If we aren't intentional on discovering, repeating, and living out who God has created us to be, we will miss the full potential of God's dream for our lives. We wrestle with the notion that we aren't enough. We consistently live in the shadow of what *could* be, hiding from our purpose and feeling less than. We believe we don't have what it takes. We think it's for someone else, not for us because our past mistakes keep us hiding in the dark, telling us we are unqualified.

How do I know this?

Because I have lived this way. Forever and ever it seems.

The shame of sexual abuse marked me with lies that God never intended for me to believe. Being told the abuse was my fault because I was too beautiful to resist turned beauty into something painful and ugly. But whether you have faced abuse like this or not, one thing I am sure of is that you have heard lies of your own. We all hear them. And we keep the shameful parts of our lives hidden, safely locked up. We are often taught from experience that self-preservation is the key to living these days because it's safer and less painful.

Or is it?

Can we fully be ourselves if we are hiding in the shame and condemnation of who we are not? Perhaps the hiding keeps us not only from being fully known, but also keeps us living small.

Who told you you are naked and don't have what it takes? Who told you there was no hope, that your past is enough to shut down your future? That you're defined by past and present situations?

Have you ever walked into a room just in time to overhear a conversation—about you? It's painful. I've done it, and the words I heard weren't so nice. Every time this happens a runaway dialogue takes over in my mind. I usually tune in, and soon enough those words begin to define my reactions and responses to everything happening in my world.

But what you may not have realized is that God Himself is talking about you right now. Behind your back, He's been talking. From before you were even a thought in your parents' mind, He's been whispering secrets about you.

He is speaking truth over you at this very moment. And truth always trumps a lie and gives you unbelievable freedom.

Your life is a reflection of the voice you listen to.

I remember the day of tryouts like it was yesterday.

I was not the most athletic person in the family, but my mom had encouraged me to try out for the track team. I was a creative, head-in-the-clouds dreamer for all of my life. I dreamed about becoming the next Mother Theresa or one of Charlie's Angels. I either wanted to change the world through love and mercy or be part of a kick butt girl team that fought for justice (not sure how much of that has changed!). I thought if I was going to be anything, that would be it.

It wasn't only that I wasn't born with athletic coordination, I basically hated any kind of sport. The only thing that appealed to me about sports were all the hot senior high guys who were involved. I'm sure my agreement to try out for track was ninety-nine percent fueled by the fact I would have increased my chances to date an athlete. I remember being so full of hope on the first day as I sauntered onto the field—and leaving the track feeling completely defeated. Not only would I never meet my future husband on the track team because of my less than stellar performance, but I came in last for every one of the track events.

Something happened as I was leaving the field that changed everything for me. I ran into the track and field coach. Feeling dejected, I gave him a quick nod, thinking he considered me as much of the loser as I knew myself to be. I was sure he could see it stamped in neon letters on my forehead. Within moments, for reasons beyond me, this man began speaking to me as though I had won every event. Even as I protested that I was sure he didn't have the right person because I just knew I hadn't made the team, he talked to me as though I still had the potential to be a winner.

Those words had power for me, and before I realized it I turned on the light switch, exposing my fear of failure and illuminating the possibilities ahead.

My downward spiral became a sea of *endless* possibility.

As the season continued, I found myself moving from fortieth place to twentieth place. I never made it to the number one spot, but I became a different person who believed what was being spoken into me. It made me want to dig deep into my potential in every area of my life.

There have been so many times in my life when I've wished I'd had that coach in my back pocket to pull him out and hear those words of encouragement over and over again. What I've discovered about life is that you get what you go after. And the words you hear in your head are a compass that directs where you go.

"Words are, of course, the most powerful drug used by mankind," said Rudyard Kipling in his speech to the Royal College of Surgeons in London in 1923. He continued, "Not only do words infect, egotize, narcotize and paralyze, but they enter into and colour the the minutest cells of the brain; they powerfully shape how a person feels and thinks, positively or negatively."[16]

The words you listen to in your head yield the power to plant seeds of either success or failure. They affect how you think, and they frame how you see yourself and your future. Words are power conductors that have been used to start wars, heal nations, launch products, restore relationships, give freedom, change patterns, and even inspire the average person next door to make history. In fact, the Bible tells us there is life and death in the words we speak.[17]

The words you are listening to in your head right now are determining everything—your direction, your confidence, and your potential.

The golden ticket for me was discovering that God is speaking life over my life all day, every day. Like my coach, He believes in me, and has not only created me with a purpose, but is constantly speaking over me all I need to walk it out.

God is the the ultimate life coach.

Right now, actually, just in the amount of time it took you to read this chapter, He has been speaking life, and He doesn't stop just because you are unaware of Him.

> *Praise be unto the God and Father of our Lord Jesus Christ*
> *who has blessed us in heavenly realms with every spiritual*
> *blessing in Christ.*
> Ephesians 1:3

The word *blessings* in Greek literally means "praise, laudation, fair speaking, an invocation of blessing or benefit." So right now, while you are reading this, God is *blessing* you, speaking into and over you His purposes for your life. Those words have the potential to flip the light on to every lie the enemy has poured into you for years.

It did for me. And still does every day. In fact, what God is speaking over you right now has the ability to bring dead, hopeless situations to life and to roll back your insecurity and charge up your *brave*.

Every word He speaks is a treasure trove of hope, wisdom, solution, training, coaching, mentoring, boatloads of mercy and grace, unconfined love, all correcting and realigning my direction. Everything you need for purpose is whispered and shouted through the Word of God, a love letter from God's heart to yours.

It's possible that the simple act of agreeing with what He is already saying has the potential to activate in you what has been in the dark because of the reverb of lies. When several thousand years ago God said, "light be," not only was the light you see created, but gamma rays, x-rays, and ultra violet rays— all light that our human eyes can't perceive—were also formed. And those two words out of God's mouth, "Light be," are *still* moving. Light is an energy source that moves at 186,282 miles per second. That means if you could travel at the speed of light you would be able to travel around the earth seven and a half times a second.

Every time the sun comes up or you feel its warmth on your skin, let it remind you that it is the product of God speaking. When you see the stars and the moon, know that their source was from just two words spoken by God: "Light be."

The action and life those words contain still enable each of us to see the world around us. Right now, God is speaking over *your* life; anything you need right now is at your disposal. His words are breathed into us with the very essence of who He is—and they don't have an expiration date.[18] And while you may not be able to see all the action behind the words He is speaking right now this doesn't mean heaven is distant.

How much of your day would change if you realized the encouragement and strength you need is already being spoken over you? And not just by a former teacher, your parents, your boss or friends, but by the One who loves you most—God?

He is declaring over you right now:

You are the head and not the tail.
Deuteronomy 28:13

He is able to do exceedingly abundantly above what you
ask or think.
Ephesians 3:20-21 KJV

He has not given you a spirit of fear but of love power and a
sound mind.
2 Timothy 1:7 KJV

Nothing is impossible with God.
Luke 1:37 NKJV

And we know that in all things for good for you who are called according to His purpose.
Romans 8:28

He has engraved you on the palms of His hands.
Isaiah 49:16

He has glorious plans and purposes for us.
Ephesians 1:11 MSG

You have the mind of Christ.
1 Corinthians 2:16

You can do ALL things through Christ who strengthens you.
Philippians 4:13

I am with you; I will give you strength and will help you.
Isaiah 41:10

# 4

# You can Reach the Light Switch

It might be a stretch, but I am confident you can reach the light switch yourself to expose the fears. For too long fear, in the form of negative thoughts and words, has lead us down the wrong path. The choice is yours, friend. God has entrusted you with the ability to choose. What will you do?

Listen, I get it! I too have *so* many issues; more issues than *Vogue* in fact (cymbal crash). I complained I had no mentors; I thought no one else had the same problems I did. I didn't feel smart enough or strong enough. If only I had more gifts, then I could turn on the switch.

Simply put, no one is going to move you toward your destiny. You have to decide you want it more than the fear keeping you from it.

Your fear is one hundred percent dependent on *you* for survival.

Choosing to listen to what God says about you above the din of lies is everything. That is when you realize that God has entrusted you with the power of choice to lead your life. It takes the label of your life from victim to leader.

For me it was a gradual step by step journey to the light switch. My crushing timidity constantly held me back. It was when I saw the girls in our church who I was responsible for leading, still trapped in the thought patterns that held them back, that I realized this circus wasn't just about me. I couldn't lead them somewhere I hadn't gone myself, and until I started changing the way I thought about myself, I would never be able to help them change the way they thought about themselves. The thought that others were dependent on my leadership awakened me; my leadership was directly tied to what I overcame.

Leading yourself is following Jesus. His perfect love removes all fear.[19] Not that we are sufficiently qualified in ourselves to claim anything as coming from us, but our sufficiency and qualifications come from God.[20]

≈

I love the following excerpt from the book *Cutting for Stone* by Abraham Verghese because it's an in-your-face challenge to not settle but instead look deeper at the glorious possibility God has placed in us:

> *I chose the specialty of surgery because of Matron, that steady presence during my boyhood and adolescence. "What is the hardest thing you can possibly do?" She said when I went to her for advice on the darkest day of the first half of my life.*
>
> *I squirmed. How easily Matron probed the gap between ambition and expediency. "Why must I do what's hardest?"*
>
> *"Because, Marion, you are an instrument of God. Don't leave the instrument sitting in its case, my son. Play! Leave no part of your instrument unexplored. Why settle for 'Three Blind Mice' when you can play the 'Gloria'?"*
>
> *How unfair of Matron to evoke that soaring chorale which always made me feel that I stood with every mortal creature looking up to the heavens in dumb wonder. She understood my unformed character.*
>
> *"But Matron, I can't dream of playing Bach, the 'Gloria'" I said under my breath. I'd never played a string or wind instrument; I couldn't read music.*
>
> *"No, Marion," she said, her gaze soft, reaching for me, her gnarled hands rough on my cheeks. "Not Bach's 'Gloria'! Yours! Your 'Gloria' lives within you. The greatest sin is not finding it, ignoring what God made possible in you."[21]*

Here's the thing many of us miss as we settle to play our own tired, *Three Blind Mice*; God Himself has entrusted us with our own *Gloria*.

*Each of us.*

And until we realize what has been entrusted to us and paid for in full by Christ, we will always live feeling like we are entitled to more, while the little rat song continues to run our lives.

You are a trust fund baby with potential and purpose. There's more value inside you than you could ever imagine. Your life has big purpose; one that involves others—not just you.

Don't ignore what God has made possible in you.

> God can do anything, you know; far more than you could ever imagine or guess or request in your wildest dreams!
> Ephesians 3:20 MSG

Gratefulness is a magnet for miracles. Instead of living in the shadow of what you feel you *don't* have, how about thanking God for what you *do* have? It's an eye opener to the treasure and grace of God in you. It attracts miracles because you now see what was "impossible" becomes "I'm possible." A recent study shows that daily gratitude for what you already have reduces stress and boosts the neurotransmitters dopamine and serotonin, giving you a sense of well being.[22] God even designed our minds to respond to a heart posture of endless possibility!

I'm excited to see what the echo of *your Gloria* will do as we begin to turn the light on together so God can use you now.

Aren't you tired of being stuck and waiting for tomorrow? Waiting to move forward? Tired of hearing who you are *not*? Weary of seeing others take off while you seemingly just stay put?

Yeah, me too.

You've been entrusted with a choice to turn on the light. It's time to stop soothing the fears and rather expose them. I'm going to take you on a journey in this book to help you expose those fears, lead yourself in God's truth, and not wait any longer for someone else to turn the light on.

In the next section we will discover what to do when we feel stuck, how to turn that feeling around, and how to stand in the authority God has already given you.

My prayer is that at the end of this book you will be ready to charge hell with a water pistol and lead with the grace to which God has called you.

### Questions to Ask Yourself:

1. *What fears have I been soothing instead of exposing? Write them down. Now find a verse in the Bible that combats these fears. Write it down as well.*
2. *In what areas do I need to lead myself?*
3. *Am I satisfied with the* Three Blind Mice *mentality, settling for less than what God designed you me? How?*
4. *What does my Gloria sound like? What are six things to describe what my life would look like if I operated in the full potential God designed for me?*

### Declaration:

I declare God's incredible blessings over my life. I will not let my past failures, doubts, or fears determine my future. I believe I have a unique, God-designed purpose and that I will live fully for what God has made possible in me. I believe nothing is impossible with God on my side!

### Prayer:

I thank you, God, that you have not given me a spirit of fear but of love power and a sound mind. That all you do is good and saturated with your unlimited love. With your help I choose to stop soothing my fears and instead expose them. I will listen to your voice above my fears. I choose to walk out the purpose for which you have created me. Thank you for divine connections and set ups to connect and grow in it. I thank you for watching over me and guiding my every step.

# PART II

# ENTRUSTED WITH PROCESS

---

*The genius thing was we didn't give up.*

— Jay Z —

---

# 5

# The First Few Steps

The first few steps into the river weren't that bad. A little chilly, sure, but just taking those steps helped to quell the terror that seemed to suffocate me.

I had never in my wildest dreams ever imagined I would be in this place. My husband and I, in our twenties and full of expectation and hope, along with our eight-month-old daughter Bethany, were on the first of many missions trips. Nestled into the Himalayan mountains, we were part of a team of forty Americans intent on backpacking Bibles into villages where people had never heard the name of Jesus. We were all excited and passionate and believed this was God's plan to impact a nation with His love.

But as excited as we were, none of us had physically prepared enough for the grueling days ahead that would include climbing creek beds and mountain paths as we traversed the nation. Nepal is one of the most breathtaking countries in the world, with its snow-capped mountains, untouched rich green valleys, and rice terraces dotting the sides of mountains. On our first day of training I found myself exhausted and completely terrified by our first challenge.

We had to cross a river.

On foot.

To top it off, it was rainy season so the usually knee deep water had risen to almost chest high with a swift, muddied current. As we made a human chain to cross, hand-in-hand, we worked to secure our footing.

We took it one step at a time, but each step was more precarious than the one before because of the thick mud base that tried to swallow our feet. With each step we fought against the current that tried to pull at our bodies.

Wedged between my husband and a friend, I started feeling a tiny bit of relief as I moved closer to the other side. Then we hit the halfway mark. The guy in front of me slipped slightly and let go of my hand.

Screaming in terror as the current pulled me down, I looked down in horror to see the body of a dead dog floating by just a few feet away from me.

As if I wasn't already thinking this would be the end of me, the passing of a lifeless animal right next to me assured my demise. As a total loss of control set in, along with my hysteria I became paralyzed when I realized I would die right there in the river.

It wasn't until I heard my husband yelling my name above the roaring current that I finally got a hold of myself. He found my hand, steadied me, and guided me back to the human chain making its way across the river.

Needless to say, I was done with rivers and hoped for a bridge the next time. But at the time, many of the rivers in Nepal didn't have adequate bridges. And if they did, they were usually made of ropes or a basket with a pulley. So the next week when we encountered another river I broke out into a cold sweat. The same fear and trepidation from the last experience took over me. I believed I would be stuck in the middle and never make it across.

I just stood there, a strong desire to turn back consuming every thought running through my mind. I was shaken out of my reverie by the guide urging me into the river. I pleaded with the four-foot Sherpa to either turn back or to carry me, but it was to no avail. His bold response to my fear surprised me. As he spoke with the authority of someone who had a ton of experience with us feeble, whiny Americans, I realized he was not only giving me a key to cross the river but also revealing to me how to not get stuck in the middle of life.

He said, "Fix your eyes on something across the river, a rock or a tree. Don't take your eyes off of that, and fight to keep the focus; then it won't matter how swift the current or how high the water is, you won't ever get stuck in the middle. You'll make it across." What he said next was pure gold. He said, "Enjoy the crossing; it makes the destination sweeter."

Enjoy the crossing; it makes the destination sweeter.

If you're human and you've had a dream for your future, you're already acquainted with the obstacles that become land mines and keep you stuck. The land mines that pepper the landscape of resistance are filled with the remnants of dreams discarded along the way. There is a dull restlessness that perhaps began as a whisper, but has become a roar you're having difficulty ignoring.

But here's my question for you: Do you have the courage to bring your dreams to reality, and to keep going, to keep showing up—not in spite of the resistance but because of it? Because honestly, the resistance is not meant to stop you or to make you feel as though you will be stuck in the middle forever. It's not meant to make you weary or feel like you don't have the right to do this.

But often it does.

We tend to look at the experience from a standpoint that we are flawed or *less than*. Perhaps it isolates you a bit, making you look at others who are taking off while you are still in the middle, fighting the current that wants to pull you into a downward spiral. But you are not alone, and when you grab hold of that concept I believe the walls and mindsets that have kept you contained will come down. You'll begin to stand in the wide open spaces you'd always hoped you would be.[23]

I know exactly how you've felt because I've been there: when the weariness and frustration of the moment you are facing make it feel as though it's almost too weighty to carry. Our culture begs us to focus on our arrival and have no patience for the process of getting there. In a world driven by goals, the trophy is given to the fastest runner in the race, the quickest achiever, often overlooking the process. We are so busy; we don't have time to wait. We desire instantaneous destination. Of course we need goals, we need a dream, we need to see something in the future to focus on and keep moving, right? Pitching a tent in what might happen one day and waiting to live fully until then is a sad way to exist.

*Beware of destination addiction: The idea that happiness is in the next place, the next job, or even with the next partner. Until you give up the idea that happiness is somewhere else, it will never be where you are.*

— Shelley Giglio —

How often do we miss the gift of joy now because it is camouflaged in the process of the present? But all of what you are facing right now is not a side note to your story; it *is* your story. God desires to use us *because* of our failure, hurt, pain, and agony, not *in spite* of it. We've been entrusted with not only a promise, but the *process*.

Perhaps we have been living our whole lives missing the point that it's not just about what we've been *entitled* to, but what we've been *entrusted* with.

You, friend, have been entrusted with gold: talents, strengths, unending purpose and possibilities…life itself. You've been uniquely entrusted with more gold than you can even begin to understand, all of it woven with threads of love from your Creator. The power of process, though, is one of the sweetest gifts you've been entrusted with by God. It has the ability to grow capacity and teach us to push past our limitations.

The problem is, the longer you are in a holding pattern on the runway, the more you begin to question or—even believe—you were created to take off.

As time passes, what was once just an obstacle becomes the muck of life that quickly swallows up dreams and any hope of a fulfilling purpose.

*That boss is outrageous; I'll never move ahead.*
*I don't even see one available spouse possibility for someone my age.*
*Those university loans seem overwhelming.*
*I would be a great mom if I could just get pregnant.*
*Will my kids ever listen and behave?*
*I want my business to just take off already.*
*Will I ever stop living paycheck to paycheck?*
*I worked hard to get my degree but am just surviving the cubicle life.*
*I want to change the world but am having a hard time making simple life decisions.*

You feel *stuck*.

I am not a good wait-er. I don't have a lot of patience for slow lines at the grocery store and seriously, just forget it if I have to wait at Starbucks

(Don't these people know my life and theirs depends on the amount of caffeine I ingest before 9 a.m.?). And believe me, navigating the massive amount of traffic we endure daily in the DC Metro area is next level waiting.

When all four of our kids were little, it seemed to take eons to get everyone dressed and out the door for a simple run for milk and diapers. The arguments and squabbles that inevitably followed the rush were enough to drive anyone mad. "Crazy Pants Mama" would appear, much to my four precious kids' chagrin. I didn't realize the process was adding valuable endurance, tenacity (and a few white hairs!) to my life.

Waiting is often the hard stuff. The not-so-glamorous, unpretty stuff. It's the day in and day out stuff.

You see, however, in hindsight I have discovered that the strength, clarity, character, and capacity that is built in the process is worth its weight in gold. I am grateful for those seasons of "not yet." Often in our culture we look at resistance and sacrifice as obstacles that makes us feel as though we will never accomplish anything in life. We think we've failed, and —we believe it, in fact—that we are less than perfect. But that resistance is there for a reason. It's an incubator that will—if you let it— increase your capacity, stretch you past your limitations, and grow your gifts and abilities to a place you never thought possible.

Guess what—you're smart! You're *very* smart and talented. You have so much to give because you are gifted, my friend. Beyond what you think, God doesn't just need you. He wants you. In fact, He chose you.

# 6

# The Not Yet Zone

Carolyn Dweck, a professor at Stanford University, did a fascinating study she called the "Power of Yet." Her work gives profound insight into the difference between a fixed mindset and the realm of *not yet*. I believe it is a powerful lesson in what happens in the middle of what we perceive to be an "I'm stuck" season.

Several years before her research, Dr. Dweck heard about a high school in Chicago that required students to pass a certain number of courses to graduate. If they didn't meet the criteria, they would receive the grade of *Not Yet*.

She loved this idea, because in a traditional classroom a failing grade would far too often define the student in life. But *Not Yet* was a learning curve that gave them a path into the future. It was a turning point in her career, as she began to study how children coped with challenge and difficulty.

She gave ten-year-olds problems that were slightly too hard for them. Some of them responded in a positive way. "I loved the challenge," they would say. They understood that their abilities could be developed; they had a *growth mindset*. Others felt it was catastrophic; they were failures from a more *fixed mindset* perspective. Dr. Dweck discovered that instead of luxuriating in the power of *not yet*, they were gripped in the tyranny of *now*. In study after study, the fixed mindset students ran from difficulty.

Scientists measured the electrical activity of the brain as students confronted an error. The students who exhibited the fixed pass/fail mentality recorded barely any new brain activity. But the students with the growth mindset, the "not yet" mindset, engaged deeply; their brain was on fire; they processed the error (the resistance), learned from it, and then corrected it.

Dr. Dweck found this bled over into many of the employers who began reaching out to her, as many of their young new recruits were quitting, or became depressed because they were facing difficulty with a fixed mindset, feeling like they were failing instead of looking for solutions to learn. Many of them looked for constant awards and validation instead of seeing the process as the prize in itself.

Perhaps our goal should not be getting the next *A* or a constant need for validation, but to embrace the process of Not Yet. This will open the door for perseverance, endurance, and strength building.

The Not Yet mentality changes the way one thinks. Studies show every time someone pushes out of his or her comfort zone to learn something new and difficult, the neurons in their brain build new and stronger connections. Students who were taught this lesson showed that those struggling boosted their grades dramatically. In one year, a kindergarten class in Harlem that had typically lower performing test scores scored in the ninety-fifth percentile on the national achievement test. Many of those kids didn't know how to properly hold a pencil when the school year began.

In another instance, a fourth grade classroom in south Bronx that was way behind in their test scores became the number one class in the state of New York on the state math test. Furthermore, in just one year a class of Native American students on a reservation went from the bottom of their district to the top. And that district included affluent sections of Seattle, so the native kids outdid the Microsoft kids!

This happened because the meaning of effort and difficulty was transformed. Before, difficulty and resistance made these students feel like giving up. But now, the resistance created new neural connections; the students became smarter by looking at the difficulty from a different perspective.[24]

Perhaps your difficulty and resistance in the middle is a growth mindset classroom that is making *you* smarter. That resistance you're feeling—the weight of the difficulty—is not a distraction from the dream; it is the path to the dream. It is designed by God to build fortitude, mastery, and inner strength.

And inner strength is what creates external power.

What if we all looked at the wait consistently as a Not Yet Zone, rather than through the eyes of whether we pass or fail? How would that change everything? Not only would your faith grow to the next level, but you'd become smarter, because that's how God designed the process!

Resistance training is essential to building muscle. It's definitely painful, but we have to choose it if we want to build muscle capacity to carry weight.

> *That is why waiting does not diminish us, any more than waiting diminishes a pregnant mother. We are enlarged in the waiting. We, of course, don't see what is enlarging us. But the longer we wait, the larger we become, and the more joyful our expectancy.*
> Romans 8:25

Where there is no struggle there is no strength. Even an airplane has to experience resistance airflow to take off. What you consider a failure is actually designed to build into you what you need to walk out the promise God has for you.

But perspective is everything. How you *view the waiting process* is everything. And it's fascinating to discover what happens during the wait, when it's not yet time.

We've often been taught in those moments that we need to change something on the outside, whether our surroundings, our friends, or our churches. But honestly, when we begin to feel that tension and that restlessness, a perspective change may be in order to allow us to see the positive changes that are happening. Perhaps what's holding us back from taking off isn't the resistance, but our view of the resistance.

What we consider a limitation is really a set up for a take-off.

# 7

# How you Wait is Everything

*Argue for your limitations and you get to keep them.*

— Melissa Gilbert —

Leah and Rachel lived a pretty comfortable (albeit, nomadic) life, if you consider living in a tent and feeding camels comfortable.[25] But in their time, it was close to working at Starbucks, having a car in the garage, and living in an upper class suburban neighborhood. Typical teenagers, both girls dreamed of getting married and couldn't wait for Mr. Right to come riding in on a white horse (or camel) and sweep them off their feet.

Rachel was the darling of the family—pretty and clever—whereas Leah plugged along being obedient, hard-working, and responsible. One day a good-looking, wealthy kinsman named Jacob showed up, looking for a haven from his brother's rage, and Leah fell in love at once. He was a catch. Though it didn't surprise Leah at all that Jacob only had eyes for Rachel, just as everyone always did. Hidden behind her sister's beauty Leah often felt ordinary, allowing that to define not only how she saw herself, but how she thought others saw her as well.

She had dreamed her whole life about Mr. Right. She read wedding magazines, planned what her married life would look like, and stared at the available guys in the market. So imagine the level of disappointment she felt when, on her sister's wedding day, not only was her younger sister marrying Jacob, but at the last minute she is thrown into the honeymoon suite instead of Rachel, deceiving her sister's husband. As if that isn't bad enough, we find out as we continue to read the story that she was totally unloved by Jacob.

No wedding celebration for Leah, no wedding showers, no dress shopping, no accolades or well wishes for a happy and long life. Just shame in knowing she was second best. She was the number two choice. She is stuck in a marriage in which she is unloved by her husband.

We've all been on a runway waiting to take off. Maybe that's where you are even now, the moment when all you feel is the silence from the air traffic control radio tower and the resistance air flow, lack of clarity, mental battles or feeling like no one sees you or hears you.

Perhaps you've ended up in a bed of circumstances you didn't ask for. Or you feel as though you are constantly the number two choice in a number one world. And in *that* place in *this* time is the biggest urge to give up.

I know; I've been there.

But we're not alone. God knew we would face moments like this, and He so wanted us to know He doesn't leave; in fact, He calls Himself *Immanuel*, which means *God with us*.

God saw Leah and knew she was unloved by her husband. And God sees you right now in your "stuck" place, in the "Hey, are you there, God?" season when we can assume He is not listening to our prayers.

Don't confuse God's patience with His absence.

I wasted so much time in the Not Yet Zone trying to figure out what I had done to cause God to leave the room. I had to realize that my sensing His presence is not based on my performance but on my belief that He exists.

> *But without faith it is impossible to please Him, for He who comes to God must believe that He is, and that He is a rewarder of those who diligently seek Him.*
> Hebrews 11:6

I love how the premise of this verse shows us a part of God's personality that we don't always see. There are so many descriptions of who He is in the Bible—He's love, the light of the world, a strong tower, and our peace. But one of my favorites is He's a *rewarder*. And if we understand that concept, everything changes. Too often in the middle of what we're walking through, we tend to believe just the beginning of this verse: *It's impossible to please him....*

Totes; I get it.

That's what I thought for most of my life too. Even though I was an avid church goer, my view of God was that His blessing, favor, and validation was based on my performance. The day the light shone on the truth was when I understood that it isn't what *I do for Him*; it's what *He did for me* two thousand years ago on the cross. I don't fight *for* victory, but *from* a place of victory already won on the cross. Therefore, everything I do for Him is a response to what He has already done for me. I no longer base it on trying to get his approval because of my perfect performance. I respond out of gratefulness for His unlimited grace and love.

How often have you kept your eyes on the mess in the middle and have missed the miracle by not keeping your eyes on the One who works the miracles? The lies we battle the most are over who God says *He is* and who God says *we are*.

And so it was with Leah. She allowed her circumstance to define who she was and how she saw God. But God saw the pain she suffered from being unloved, so He made sure she was the first to have a baby.

In biblical times babies were named around the season the parents were experiencing. Leah's first son was named Reuben, which means *God has seen my misery*; and *a sign that now my husband will love me*. Her thoughts were *maybe now God sees me and things are going to change*. She defined herself as unloved and God as one who's blurry vision was potentially clearing up. Maybe there was a glimmer of hope, but she was not convinced.

Leah had a second son whom she named Simeon, meaning *God has heard that I was unloved and so he gave me this son also; maybe now God hears and things are going to change*. But she wasn't convinced, because when her third son was born she named him Levi, which means *maybe now my husband will connect with me*.

Can you imagine every time she called those boys for dinner? Reuben (*I am unloved and maybe God sees me*), Simeon (*I am still unloved and maybe God will open his eyes to see now*), and Levi (*I am still unloved and alone*). I can only imagine how depressing that dinner table conversation was!

She named her boys—and her situation. Maybe you haven't named your children after your heartbreak, but I am sure you have at some point—like me—named yourself after your situation.

"I am hopeless."

"I am so alone."

"I am a failure."

"I am second best in a number one world."

It was between her third and fourth son when Leah began to experience a personal transformation. The Bible doesn't tell us what happened, but I believe somewhere in the middle of the birth of her sons her mindset changed. She started looking at her misery and despair through different eyes, instead of focusing on the mess she was in, and through the eyes of the One who works miracles.

She went from a *fixed mindset* of failure to an *endless possibilities mindset* in which she finally saw God in her Not Yet Zone.

And *that* perspective is everything.

We are often caught without understanding in the here and now.

Caught in the space between beginnings and endings.

Feeling a bit blinded and insecure in our present place within the human experience. But it's not about your current surroundings friend, it's about Who you see and hear in the Not Yet.

# 8

# What you See is who you Become

When Pinin Brambilla Barcilon conducted the most recent restoration of the *The Last Supper* by Leonardo Da Vinci, she discovered years of mold, glue, repaint, and smog had collected on the surface of the original painting. After twenty years of painstakingly detailed work, Pinin Barcilon and her team were able to reveal the expressive and chromatic intensity of the painting that was believed to have been lost forever. In fact, the luminosity of the original painting was regained.[26]

God made you, a masterpiece, one of His crowning creations. Every part of who you are is a celebration of His love. He created you in His image, radiating the luminosity of His life.

Too often what was once the original design is covered over by the debris of a pass/fail mindset that hides the genius of what He has created us for. A simple perspective change can turn a pass fail mindset into a growth mindset classroom.

There were three pass/fail mindsets that kept Leah stuck; that locked her into a fixed world, instead of one full of endless possibilities. If you're anything like me, you've encountered them as well, and if they're not addressed they will mess with your identity. Recognizing them is the key to breaking free and seeing the magnificent underpinnings of what God wired into us.

*Pass/Fail Mindset 1: Comparison*

For years, I compared myself to the people I admired—people who were so confident, gifted, and carried themselves with a natural effervescence. These people were doing all the cool stuff I dreamed of doing and were far more successful than me. I imagined these "successful" people had things I didn't. Financial resources, the right connections, a greater ability to focus, teams of hundreds of brilliant people they lead with pure genius.

All of what they had was seemingly just beyond my reach. The times I would muster up enough confidence to walk into a room, it would quickly disintegrate into a paralyzed state of fear and insecurity. As I measured myself, I was always the *less than* contributor.

In fact, even as I sit here writing I face a huge mental battle. I've had major focus issues (Oooh...look! There's a bird!) that often go something like this: I get up at the crack of dawn to finish writing a chapter. Thirty minutes into writing, I see an ad for a great pair of shoes at Nordstrom online. I check them out. They're on sale (!!). Now, I am totally distracted and think I should just go get a cup of coffee. I then notice the dishwasher needs to be emptied and filled. Hmm...I'm hungry now; I should probably eat.... By the time I got back to my desk to write, an hour and a half has already passed.

And the cycle of comparison continues. *Real writers don't struggle like this. Is anyone even going to want to read this?*

But where does this mindset come from?

I believe it begins with a scarcity mentality.[27] Our worthiness is directly connected to it. The *I am not enough* thoughts do laps in our mind like an Olympic marathon runner. Some of us have become so good at this that the track is imbedded into who we really believe we are. We measure our self-worth and value on what others have and what we appear to lack.

*I would be worthy if I was skinnier.*
*I would be worthy if I could hold my marriage together.*
*I would be worthy if he called and asked me out.*
*I would be worthy if I had more degrees.*
*I would be worthy if everyone thought I was a good parent.*

And why do we feel we are failing at all of this? Because we've seen someone else on another runway taking off, and it looks so incredible and beautiful and our basic insecurities say we want what they have.

Our self-worth is often tied to our performance, achievement, and productivity. All of us deal with this, and just as it begins to simmer down a bit, our culture reminds us through the savvy marketing of photo-shopped cover girls and fancy cars that we have a huge, looming, impossible mountain to climb in order to keep up with the Joneses!

What begins as a simple expression of the crazy busy life, or even the difficult life filled with challenge after challenge, grows into a justification for an *unfulfilled* life.[28]

The reason for the tension is because God has hardwired us to desire love and connection and not the constant dissatisfaction of the *not enough* in the Not Yet Zone.

If we are not careful we will live life tied up in "nots."

The abundant, more-than-enough life with Him is what God envisions for you. And in this life we are never left feeling shortchanged. Quite the contrary—we can't round up enough containers to hold everything God generously pours into our lives through the Holy Spirit.[29]

Once I stopped wasting time and energy getting lost in what I now call *comparison hangovers* and started taking consistent action, I realized something big.

All of my thoughts about what "successful" people had that I didn't were big fat lies—and I was the one making excuses to stay where I was!

The truth is, I was scared I was not good enough. I had limited myself, my capabilities, and my worth as a human being. But in reality, I had everything I needed to pull myself up and succeed in Christ.

And it's the same for you. You are capable of reaching your full potential. It doesn't matter how much time, money, or experience you think you lack; you were born with everything you need to reach your highest creative possibility. You can do all things through Christ who strengthens you![30]

What holds most of us back are excuses; excuses about why other people can do things that we can't. I'm not sure about you, but I have spent too many years with the comparison handicap, wanting to be someone else. It wasn't until I realized that when I really made God number one, by believing what He said *about* me and what He had done *for* me, that I settled into a confident number two spot—confident that He is watching over and guiding my every step.

### Pass/Fail Mindset 2: Condemnation

As a three-year-old, I was told by the abuser it was my fault I was sexually abused because I was "too beautiful" to resist. This experience set me on a life course that allowed shame and condemnation to keep hidden the biggest part of God's story wrapped in mine.

Condemnation, if not addressed, works in tandem with comparison[31] to keep you from seeing what you've been entrusted with. You see, shame lives here. It speaks to our identity. It's all about the fear of losing connection and keeps us in a fixed mindset of failure. And we don't want anyone to see our failure because we risk losing their connection and validation. We constantly live under the weight of shame—a key point to remember as we move forward.

The past is a point of reference, not a residence.

Abuse and shame kept me living in the past and the redemption part of my story locked up and hidden. I lived under the tyranny of condemnation; guilt was my constant companion. Guilt said I *did* something bad, while shame said I *am* bad. Willingness to be vulnerable with your imperfections is what opens the door not only to healing but to silencing the voice of condemnation.

> *There is therefore no condemnation in Christ.*
> Romans 8:1

None. Nada. Zero. Doesn't matter what language; it all means the same. If negative self-doubt and self-criticism is talking to you, that's not language God speaks; it's the shadow of a lie. It's time to change what dialogue we listen to.

It's time to stop performing autopsies on your failures. You can't move forward always looking in the rear view mirror.

"You are imperfect and you are hardwired for struggle, but you are worthy of love and belonging"[32] but until we realize this, we will remain stuck in the Not Yet Zone. Making mistakes is better than faking perfections. You've got incredible gifts, skills, and costly wisdom wired into you from those mistakes. And remember, those scars and cracks are not just an integral part of your story; they *are* your story.

Want to be happy? Stop trying to be perfect. Those who have a strong sense of love and belonging have the courage to be imperfect. You will never be happy until you realize you will never be perfect. The perfect love that comes from God[33] is the only thing that can give us the courage to be imperfect.

There is only One who is perfect. And His name is Jesus.

As a recovering perfectionist, I can tell you it's a self-destructive lifestyle and, honestly, addictive. It fuels the primary thought: *If I look perfect and do everything perfectly I can avoid or minimize the painful feelings of shame, judgment and condemnation And everyone will love me.*[34] This becomes a vicious cycle that hides who we really are.

Shame's energy source forces us into a cave of hiding and silence. That's why it loves perfectionists; it's easy to keep us quiet. Shame is silenced when we say, "This hurts; this is disappointing and maybe even devastating."

My value is not found in striving for success or approval but in my constant invitation for God to redeem every weak area. It's not a cover up, a hope to, or even a wish list; it's an invitation for transformation. When I am weak I get to see *His* strength.

Understanding the value He places on us is life changing; that in Him I am *enough*.

Perhaps perfection looks different to God than it does to us. God says He will perfect that which concerns us.[35] So perfect to me, means He's faithful to bring order to my chaos; He'll make everything work out so that I look "perfectly perfect."

Here's what I've found in the last few years that has begun to unravel the power of condemnation and set a course of daily freedom.

First I must identify with the fact I am not perfect nor will I ever be. (an a-ha moment right there!) We are always imperfect. He is always perfect. When I invite Him into my imperfection, His perfection redeems it: turns it around, heals and restores, and uses the place where my imperfect story intersects with the power of His grace and redemption. When we change our internal dialogue from *what will people think?* to *I am enough* in Him, we see God's story marking ours. Perfectionism can become the enemy of good *enough* and *done*.

We will not finish (or even start) something if we are cornered into believing it's not worth it if it's not perfect.

Some of the most powerful teaching moments are the ones in which you screw up. What God is bringing you through in this very moment will be the testimony that brings somebody else through—no mess, no message. Often God is more concerned with the battle He wants to win *in* you than the one you want Him to win *for* you.

When He is invited in, it's amazing what changes. Your fear of vulnerability, of being a *two* fades. Because unless He's *one*, nothing else matters.

## Pass/Fail Mindset 3: Confidence

*No one can make you feel inferior without your consent.*

— Eleanor Roosevelt —

I was lying in bed, ready to fall into a blissful sleep after a very full day. All of a sudden I realized my wedding ring was missing from my finger. As panic began to flood over me, I thought back through the day; I couldn't imagine where I could have left it. *Could I possibly have thrown it away?* Now fully awake I darted into the kitchen, horrified to find the boys had taken the trash to the back alley. Without thinking twice, I ran out to the alley and began pulling the trash apart. The value was not just the money my husband had paid for my ring, but the value of the relationship it represented. After many minutes of scrounging through the garbage bag, I uncovered my ring, wrapped in a mayo-covered paper towel. I was in tears.

*So do not throw away your confidence it will be richly rewarded.*
Hebrews 10:35

How often do we throw away our confidence without a second thought? We fear being vulnerable with our lives because we live with a pass/fail mentality that shuts us down from even thinking we can rise up and move forward. The fact that God tells us in the Bible to not throw away our confidence because of the reward attached to it, is a reminder of the value He has placed on our confidence.

*If we are not careful we will trade our authenticity for approval and begin hustling for acceptance. Authenticity is the daily practice of letting go of who we think we're supposed to be and embracing who we are. Choosing authenticity means cultivating the courage to be imperfect, to set boundaries, and to allow ourselves to be vulnerable exercising the compassion that comes from knowing that we are all made of strength and struggle. Nurturing the connection and sense of belonging that can only happen when we believe that we are enough. At the end of the day you either walk inside your story and own it or you stand outside your story and hustle for your worthiness.*[36]

— Brene Brown —

All of us do it. As a former approval hustler, I have discovered the most freeing thing is learning how to be vulnerable and authentically true to who we are. And it's a choice and a process to allow that discovery make us braver by coming clean with our story.

And if we own our story than we can write the ending.

Be your own ruthless editor, only allowing in the perception that builds your confidence. At some point you have to decide you aren't going to let insecure thoughts ruin something amazing by becoming the narrative of your story. You are good enough, smart enough, beautiful enough, and strong enough; believe it and never let insecurity run your life. Insecurity is not your boss.

*Be content with who you are and don't put on airs. God's strong hand is on you; He will promote you at the right time. Live carefree before God; He is most careful for you.*
1 Peter 5:6-7

The way you define your life determines your destiny, so don't let the opposition, failure, condemnation, or comparison define you; let God's words define you. He's the One with the authority to tell you who you are!

# 9

# How it's Going Doesn't Determine how you're Doing

Somewhere along the way, our friend Leah became resolute on who God was in the wait. She was no longer naming her children according to her situation, but she began naming the grace she saw in the middle of the wait.

To be *resolute* is to be loosened back from all hindrances to accomplishing something. When you become resolute, even though nothing from your circumstances has changed, you are loosening yourself from all hindrances that hold you back.

Leah was no longer defined by comparison, condemnation, and lack of confidence. Her shame and situation no longer defined her either.

Leah had a fourth son, whom she named Judah, meaning, *This time I will praise the Lord.*

*This time, I will thank God.*

*This time is different; I will make God bigger than my circumstance.*

*This time, while I am still waiting to be loved, valued, noticed by my husband, I won't forget about the One who loves me most.*

*This time, the resistance in life I feel is going to make me stronger.*

*This time, I am enjoying my life*—not *in spite of* but *because of* the resistance.

This time when Leah called the boys for dinner, she ended with, *This time I will see God bigger than my circumstances.*

Brain research tells us when we actually *speak out loud* what we are grateful for and name the positives of what we see even in a negative situation, it reduces stress and boosts the neurotransmitters dopamine and serotonin, which give you a sense of well being.[37] Naming your Not Yet Zone a place of *endless possibilities* actually makes you healthier *and* smarter!

Shoot. Say it out loud!

God's even wired your brain to respond when you praise God—connecting with Him and acknowledging His goodness and greatness—in the Not Yet Zone.

This time I choose a *not yet* mindset of endless possibilities. What about you? How are *you* waiting? What have you done or experienced in the past that you've allowed to define you? Your identity does not come from your struggles; your identity comes from God!

Often the circumstances in your life that hold you back are simply thought patterns that no longer work. Change the pattern and change your life.

> So what do you think? With God on our side like this, how can we lose? Is there anything He wouldn't gladly and freely do for us? The one who died for us and was raised to life for us in the presence of God at this very moment sticking up for us! What wedge can come between us?
> I am absolutely convinced—resolute, to be exact—that nothing— nothing living, nothing dead, angelic, or demonic, today or tomorrow, high or low, thinkable or unthinkable—absolutely nothing can come between us because of the way Jesus our Master has embraced us
> Romans 8:31-39.

Planes only take off because of their resistance factor. Stop going back into the hangars of life and waiting for the resistance to pass.

Time to stay on the runway and speak the truth to yourself:

*This time I won't question His patience for His absence.*

*This time I look at the past as a place of reference not residence.*

*This time I know God hears and sees me.*

*This time comparison, shame, and condemnation don't define me; God's plan and purpose does.*

*This time, I have authority. So this time I will praise you.*

*This time I have been entrusted with the resistance.*

*This time it's not pass or fail; I am not letting the resistance stop me, but propel me.*

Job declared at the end of the most difficult thing he ever faced:

> *I'm convinced: You can do anything and everything. Nothing and*
> *no one can upset your plans. I admit I once lived by rumors of you;*
> *now I have it all firsthand—from my own eyes and ears!*
> (Job 42:3-6 MSG)

It's in the hard places where you discover who God is for yourself, no longer living off the rumors of what others say. You must know He is *for* you and *not against* you. You must know how greatly loved you are—not because of your pass/fail performance but because of who He is.

> *Define yourself as one radically loved by God. This is your true self,*
> *every other identity is an illusion.*[38]
>
> — Brennan Manning —

If you discover the sweetness of an intimate relationship and friendship with the One who loves you most in the process, you've discovered pure gold.

God has you in an incubator. It's uncomfortable; it makes you want to give up. But I want you to keep going. The world needs what you have. And you need the resistance because what you have to offer is being refined right here in this place. This time. Don't give up; choose to see what God sees in you and not what your experiences want to tell you.

You've got this, friend; I believe in you and so does heaven. You can do it. You are in a magnificent Not Yet Zone and I believe God has amazing things in store for you in this season. In the next section you'll learn about how God has already written the "brave" you need into your story to see the turnaround you've been hoping for.

### Questions to Ask Yourself:

1. *Have I been looking at my current situation as a pass/fail or a Not Yet Zone?*
2. *In what areas has the shame of my past or present tried to define me?*
3. *In what areas do I need to become resolute?*

Take a few minutes to write down some things you're grateful for in this present moment. Then speak them out loud daily for twenty-one days. Feel free to add to the list, but be consistent. Be sure to include gratitude for the Not Yet Zone you are in!

### Declaration:

I declare I have the grace I need for today and every day. Nothing I face this day will be too much for me. With Christ I can do all things, overcome every obstacle, outlast every challenge, and come through difficulty better off than I was before. This time I will praise God, not in spite of, but because of my circumstances that are making me wiser and stronger and more resolute. I am an overcomer in Christ.

### Prayer:

God, I thank you that you haven't left me alone in this place and that you are present. That whether I feel your love or not, I choose to believe it is without limitation and is not based on my performance but on yours on the cross. I agree with what what you say, that I am getting stronger, smarter, more patient, and that my potential is not decreasing but increasing in capacity and abilities. Thank you God that you are with me and that together we will see your potential and purpose in me come to pass. I give my life completely and wholly to you!

# PART III

# ENTRUSTED WITH BRAVE

---

*Your time as a caterpillar has expired; your wings are ready.*

— Author Unknown —

---

# 10

# Put On your Brave

It was one of those perfectly crisp fall mornings when every one of your senses comes alive. Jacks, a photographer who brilliantly captures the exquisite beauty and vision I have for our annual women's conference, and I had been walking through the sites he had scouted out as a possible location for our next photo shoot. This time, though, it wasn't a theme we were trying to capture but a bold declaration of what was in the heart of God for the girls in the DC Metro area. It was something I had personally experienced and so wanted to see these girls marked with in their own journey.

As we walked down one of the wooded paths at the National Arboretum, an oasis in the middle of DC, we stopped for a minute at a place he found that would be perfect for the images. As we stood there, I could see the leaves dappled with sunlight, dancing in the light breeze. I even heard the birds chirping, which felt a little like heaven on earth since we live in the concrete jungle of DC. I could picture the models standing there, with beautiful fierceness, bow and arrows in their hands—strong, purposed… does anyone else get caught up in a daydream and lose track of your physical surroundings for a moment?

Yeah, me too.

As I took in this "brave" picture and began to follow Jacks to the next location, I tripped over a stick on the ground. Historically, I am not known for my stellar coordination, so to avoid a complete face plant I tried to kick the stick out of the way. It was at that very moment I realized the stick was already moving.

My moment of confusion quickly melted into terror as I realized it wasn't a stick after all, but a long, black snake slithering down the path!

I don't particularly love anything from any part of the amphibian family, and have been known to go a bit out-of-my-mind-crazy if one of these creatures is anywhere near me, which is why I immediately darted down the path out of control and screaming at the top of my lungs.

How could I have envisioned a brave image in my mind one moment and then run away in terror the next?

That was not the bravest or proudest moment of my life, but in actuality, I do this a lot. You see, I love to daydream, but often the brave picture I envision—when I make the move to start a new program, connect with the right people, start a conversation, or write a book—never materializes when I'm scared off by the obstacles that inevitably show up. I get stuck in the present and don't see God's story indelibly marking the moment.

Often it's in *this* moment when you don't feel you have what it takes, or the "brave" needed to push through. I'd often shrink from what was possible because of the looming impossibility that required me to step up.

My seeming smallness and cowardice would scream at me, paralyzing any potential for forward momentum.

Can you relate?

Here's what you should know: the simple recognition that God has already written brave into the narrative of your story gives courage to your bones. It gives grace to the wait. It gives definition to the Not Yet Zone. It tells you there is a purpose for where you are right now and that it won't last forever. If you can begin to define yourself by how He sees you and not by your past or present or the length of the middle, you will begin to live in the incredible world of turnarounds.

Bravery is not the absence of fear, but the exposure of fear—then pushing through it. Courage is taking those first steps even when you can't see the path. The first step to moving forward is recognizing God as an author and finisher; offering Him the blank slate, the new chapter, or even the imperfect pages you wish you could edit out is the best invitation you could ever make.

The story of Esther is the ultimate princess story. But the more I study and obsess over it, the more I realized it's not a tale of a princess or queen entitled to what she has been given, but the most magnificent story of a woman entrusted with much and poised to make a turnaround. We aren't talking a pink, sparkly princess party (which is always fun, right?), but an everyday person like you and me who encountered a choice that would set the trajectory of her life and change the course of history. It's a story of how she chose to rise above the circumstances of the middle of her story and see beyond her own limitations to fulfill God's incredible purpose through her.

This story is about worrying less on fitting into a cookie cutter glass slipper and more about shattering the glass ceilings that hold you back.

> *Courage is not simply one of the virtues but the form of every virtue at the testing point.*

> — C. S. Lewis —

Tucked between the chronicles of kings and the thundering of prophets, is a story of someone sitting quietly, not even realizing her seemingly obscure potential until she opens her mouth. This is a story that shouts "You have a destiny, not in spite of your circumstances but because of them!" It speaks boatloads of how God is intricately entwined with every area of our lives, even in the silence when it appears heaven isn't listening and there is no answer. When there is no obvious miracle, and when the silence is louder than anything—that's when we need to listen up and pay attention.[39]

It's about your destiny and what God has planned, even in the wait, the stuck, and the silence. I just wonder how many of you have been betrayed, misled, or duped into believing a lie? We can talk ourselves right out of the purpose of God in our lives when we listen to those negative voices, and if we're not careful we can protect ourselves right out of our calling.

You see, your story is never meant to be overlaid with lies, but undergirded with truth. And the truth is, the end of your story is beyond good. And so is the middle, *and* the beginning. If we could see what God sees, I believe we would begin talking ourselves into becoming the brave person God already knows us to be.

It's understanding whether you feel it or not, God has already written brave into the narrative of your story.

Much like Esther, we all have some handicap or insufficiency that keeps us from moving forward. It stops us more than we would like to admit. But here's the deal. It doesn't stop the overlay of grace He has already positioned into your story. Remember, *you* have the potential and the courage to activate the brave in your story. It's a leadership story of the grandest kind about how to bravely lead yourself before leading anyone else.

And maybe you haven't won a beauty pageant or any other pageant ever. Nor even had a desire to. Maybe your back story is set as far from the palace as you can imagine.

But maybe—just maybe—you can still find yourself in Esther's story.

I did.

One day at the end of time, I hope we will be able to see this story replay on heaven's movie screen. It's filled with love, passion, intrigue and action. I love hero stories in which the protagonist overcomes amidst great setbacks and resistance and this one is all that.

# 11

# A Profile of Courage

If we were to open a small window into Esther's life, we'd see a young orphan girl raised by her uncle, Mordecai, in Persia—a long time ago in the times of opulent kings and lavish palaces. When it was discovered that King Ahuesarus was looking for a new queen, Mordecai felt compelled to enter Esther into the running of a beauty pageant to win the king's heart. Immediately upon seeing Esther, the king fell in love with her

It sounds like an epic fairy tale: Esther became King Ahuesarus' wife and is put on center stage for all of Persia to watch. Esther's obscure Jewish upbringing hadn't prepared her to be the leading lady in Persia, but her inner beauty and strength opened a door that would forever change history. She was the least likely to win the king's heart, yet God positioned *her* heart for this moment. It was clearly a set up for a future circumstance.

Not too long into Esther's reign, a national decree was announced for a genocide of epic proportions to annihilate all the Jewish race in Persia. It was a hopeless moment for God's people, and the majority of the population had no voice or platform to protest this travesty. But as always, God had a plan that didn't require the voice of the majority—just one obscure voice He handpicked from before time, the least likely one.

An orphan who was positioned in a palace for this moment, Queen Esther.

God picked her.

Maybe you're one who's always waiting to be picked for the team, for the job, for marriage, or for parenthood. Or perhaps you don't feel like your "obscure" voice can make a difference. Maybe you're more terrified in this moment that He *might* pick you, and you're hiding in the shadows of "what can I possibly offer?"

Whether you realize it or not, God has already handpicked you for a very unique and specific role in history, just like He did Esther.

It was intriguing for me to discover that the book of Esther is one of only two books in the Bible named after a woman (Ruth being the other) and the only one that does not mention the name of God once. And yet His story is all over it; a profound story of turnaround and redemption that God had already determined and set up for this woman.

An epic tale of choosing to be brave. Like Esther, your current choices determine the future you live. In fact, the choices you made last year are the place you live today. And not only the choices, but your thoughts, your beliefs, and the words you speak are a compass that sets the direction of your life.

But what Esther didn't realize, and what you may not realize yet either, is that God has already written the turnaround in your story. He is already in your future. And it's your yes response that sets up the turnaround. Even when your yes is a scared one, you'll discover God is ahead of you, already having turned the tables in your favor.

*Perhaps this is the moment for which you have been created.*
Esther 4:14

"Donna." I couldn't believe I was up next. I felt like crying and vomiting all at the same time. As I walked numbly to the front of the class, I already knew this wouldn't end well. I had rehearsed the failure over and over in my mind and I was sure it would be close to the very worst thing that would ever happen in my life. To make matters worse, I had to follow Anthony, who had just delivered his report with the confidence of a presidential candidate.

I had to speak in front of my whole class of fifth graders and share my report on lizards. I didn't even like lizards. Seriously, does anyone besides nine-year-old boys like lizards? I still can feel the pain I experienced as I stood there, my face warm and flushed. Could anyone else hear my heart beating as loudly as I did?

Then the most horrible thing happened.

I forgot everything I was going to say. In fact, if you had asked me my name in that moment I'm pretty sure I wouldn't have remembered that either.

So I just stood there—for what felt like hours. The longer I stood the more paralyzed I became. Any thread of courage I had was gone, as hot tears began to well up in my eyes and fall down my cheeks.

That's right. In front of thirty classmates I began to cry. I looked pleadingly at the teacher, hoping to hear her say "It's ok, Donna; you're so brilliant, we don't even need to hear your report. Go ahead and sit down."

Or at the very least could the earth please swallow me up right then, or a tornado conveniently rip through the classroom alleviating me of this pressure? Anything was better than what I was experiencing in that moment.

Panicking, I fumbled for some words... "Lizards are green..." But in my head I thought, *umm, are they green?*

One of my classmates started laughing, and another one called out, "Donna is a scaredy pants!" Within thirty seconds the entire class was chanting it: "Donna is a scaredy pants!"

Now I look back on that moment with a chuckle. Having had four kids, I've often been reminded that middle school sucks. Everyone is insecure and most are pretty mean. But that line, "Donna is a scaredy pants," stuck with me for most of my life on repeat at every turn. Fear marked me good. I look back now at the opportunities I missed, the God moments I overlooked because "Donna is a scaredy pants" was what I heard instead.

Please realize that *you* are responsible for what you hear in your head and that *you* have the ability to change it.

You must come to the place where you stop waiting for someone else to do it for you. You must get comfortable enough to take off the scaredy pants and put on your big girl panties. And it's not like hopping over to Victoria's Secret to pick up a pair; there's a bit of intentionality wrapped up in it. It's a choice; a choice that says "I am *not* going to let fear mark me any longer."

What if we saw fear as an indicator and not an intimidator?

Charles Stienmatz was an electrical engineer of towering intellect. After he retired, he was asked by a major appliance manufacturer to locate a malfunction in their electrical equipment. None of the manufacturer's experts had been able to locate the problem. Stienmatz spent some time walking around and testing the various parts of the machine complex. Finally, he took out of his pocket a piece of chalk and marked an *X* on a particular part of one machine. The manufacturers were amazed to discover the defect lay precisely where Stienmetz's chalk mark was located. Some days later, the manufacturer received a bill from Steinmetz for ten thousand dollars. They protested the amount and asked him to itemize it. He sent back an itemized bill.

> *Making one chalk mark*    *$1*
> *Knowing where to place it*    *$9,999*[40]

Knowing where to place the *X* is boss.

If you know where the chalk mark goes, the most overwhelming tasks are easily solved. If you don't, even simple tasks can be paralyzing. Perhaps the mark of fear on your life is exposing something you didn't even know was there. Instead of trying to squash the mark of fear, look at what it's covering up. Could it be that the mark of fear is revealing the clarity to what God is asking you do to?

Perhaps behind your greatest fear is your greatest calling.

It's been said that everything you've ever wanted is on the other side of fear. But I believe it goes further than that. It's the reason why turning the light on to expose your fears is more than just you seeing what's in the room.

Maybe *X* does mark the spot.

Perhaps instead of using fear as a reason to stop, we should look at it as a sign post indicating the direction we should go.

It was like that for me. I was so painfully shy; I would cross the street rather than run into someone I knew and be forced to have a conversation. The thought of speaking in public had me permanently dressed in my scaredy pants. Year after year. Those pants needed washing and removing, but they seemed to keep me "safe" and protected.

If we are not careful we can protect ourselves right ourselves right out of our calling. I know this is true because my greatest fear of speaking publicly—or speaking at all—is now my greatest calling. It's been a journey for sure. And there are still times when "Donna is a scaredy pants" replays in my mind, but I've learned to do it scared.

Then I remember my destiny is not about me or about the validation of my self-importance. It is always connected to someone else who needs to find their calling and significance. God has an amazing way of making sure all our stories connect and build upon each other. It's one of the reasons the enemy fights so hard with fear.

In any given moment you have two options, to step forward into courage and growth or to step back into fear and safety.

What fear of yours is that *X* covering up in your life, friend? What intimidating thoughts keep you from seeing what God has for you here?

# 12

# You have to Take Brave

*You gain strength, courage and confidence by every experience in which you really stop to look fear in the face. You must do the thing you think you cannot do.*

— Eleanor Roosevelt —

Esther had a choice to make. And so do you. I believe right now you might be one brave decision away from one of the most important discoveries of your entire life. Take the courage offered by looking to see what's hiding behind that *X* of fear.

Recently someone paid for my drink at Starbucks, but I was so distracted with social media on my phone that I forgot to pick it up. Who leaves a free cappuccino on the counter?

Apparently I do.

And just like that cup of free deliciousness, we can easily let distractions keep us from the free gift of courage that is offered to us from God.

Perhaps you don't even know it's there on the counter waiting for you. Too often we don't realize we will never be placed in a situation where God hasn't already offered us the courage it takes to be at the table.

Just in case you missed that, you will never ever be in a situation where God doesn't offer you courage or the "brave" you need to succeed. In scripture, often the first words out of God's mouth are, "Take courage."

He spoke to Peter as he stepped out of the boat and onto the water; when Paul faced so much adversity in a prison, God offered him the courage to know the circumstances wouldn't get easier, but that He was taking him to Rome to testify.

And so it is throughout history.

Rosa Parks made the choice to take "brave" and sit on a bus in one of the most turbulent times during the Civil Rights Movement. She said "I have learned over the years that when one's mind is made up, this diminishes fear; knowing what must be done does away with fear."[41]

Amelia Earhart chose to take "brave" and fly across the Atlantic Ocean alone. As she prepared to do what no woman had ever done before her, she said, "Courage is the price that life exacts for granting peace."[42]

Corrie Ten Boom took "brave" as she and her family helped many Jews escape the Holocaust in Nazi Germany. Corrie and her sister were sent to a concentration camp where they suffered horrific atrocities. She said, "Never be afraid to trust a unknown future to an known God."[43]

Nelson Mandela, who helped bring an end to apartheid in South Africa amidst great personal sacrifice and opposition, said, "I learned that courage was not the absence of fear, but the triumph over it. The brave man is not he who does not feel afraid, but he who conquers that fear."[44]

These were everyday people like you and me. They didn't have a special brave DNA strand that made it any easier for them than it does for you; what generated the brave was choice.

Being a mom requires brave choices daily. Sometimes when my kids were young I just had to convince myself that all four of them would succeed in life and not end up living in my basement when they were forty. Every day life had me questioning the validity of those thoughts.

"Please put your pants on before leaving the house," I'd say to my five-year-old who loved running naked in the house. "Who did you say you were with last night?" I'd constantly ask my teenagers, knowing full well that often teenagers—including mine—have moments of "not remembering" the truth. "Why are you sledding down the front steps into the street filled with traffic?" I had to inquire after a record snowfall on Capitol Hill. "Did you remember underwear in your suitcase?" I reminded my favorite ten-year-old son who needed to be told that wearing the same clothes for ten days was gross as he packed for summer camp.

As a mom, I wanted to keep my children wrapped up close to me all the time. I think too often our parenting becomes filled with fear and suspicion instead of grace and faith. To take the courage and brave being offered in the everyday life of parenting requires daily choices that affect everything. Trusting that we can parent *with* God, who is the ultimate Father keeps us believing that God can turn anything around.

Perhaps taking the "brave" offered to you looks like facing a terrifying health issue or uncertain finances. Or it's having that painful conversation, or maybe just keeping silent and relinquishing control. Sometimes the "brave" you need is to just not give up and stay the course when nothing seems to change. Remember we are the ones who choose to be a prisoner of our past or a courageous pioneer of our future. For far too long we have allowed who we were talk us out of who we are becoming. It is important for you to realize that your future is directly connected to your "brave" choices today.

You have a calling. A purpose. And you are here for a reason; more than just for yourself. You are a trailblazer and you are hardwired to be the change, which is why mediocre feels like a prison sentence and you feel the nudge for more.

It's not comfortable. It's like trying to fit into your jeans in January after binge eating Christmas cookies during the holidays. You've stretched, but the pants haven't. And so it is now. You've grown and that fear doesn't fit you any longer.

Time to move on, friend.

# 13

# Break the Code

If you look closely behind every success story—every product we love, the clothes we wear, and the food we eat—you'll find a pattern that was adhered to. (Remind me to tell you about the time I made all my clothes *without* a pattern and why you'll *never* see a picture of me from that era!) What if there was a code or pattern for success? The Bible is full of them; everything from generosity that breaks the cycle of poverty to the consistent patterns of love and forgiveness for healing relationships. The list goes on.

And so it is for being brave. If we look closely at the book of Esther, we'll see a pattern that marks the story. In fact, this pattern marks every story in the Bible; it's like a secret code that opens your faith and destiny.

I don't profess to be a literary giant; my favorite subjects in high school were lunch and art, in that order. But I found this one discovery fascinating, and knowing this has significantly marked my life and I think it will yours too.

The book of Esther was written in a literary style called Chiastic Structure. It literally means an "inverted parallelism." Sounds a bit *Star Trek*-y, but it was a common practice back in the day.

Chiastic Structure. Go ahead and say it out loud; just let that roll around on your tongue for a few minutes. We hear speeches and see movies written with the same structure today. Everything from *Star Wars* and *Frozen* to my favorite, *Pride and Prejudice* are written in this structure.

(Yes, even Mr. Darcy wasn't just charismatic, but chiastic!) It's the classic hero journey. It simply means a reversal or a turning of the tables. For instance, "Do we eat to live or live to eat?" (I'd have to answer that as a solid *yes*. Period. Eating is my super power.)

Or when John F. Kennedy remarked, "Ask not what your country can do for you, but what you can do for your country." Notice the slight reversal that changes the full meaning? God's story is chiastic too.

> *God made him who had no sin to be sin for us so that in him we can become the righteousness of Christ.*
> 2 Corinthians 5:21

The whole story of God—the greatest love story of how God turned the tables for humanity, the most significant turnaround ever—is written in Chiastic Structure. It shows how God can take our imperfections and daily failures and turn them around to build our capacity, gifts, and strengths, to use His story of grace to bring healing not only to us but others is His perfection personified.

Redemption for humanity is chiasma at its ultimate. In fact, Jesus's family history has prostitutes, murderers, liars, and cheaters (sounds like an episode of *Scandal*, huh?). But each name listed in Matthew 1 is the subject of a poignant story of a grand turnaround. Not one of those people listed deserved to be in the genealogy of the Son of God. In reality there was a lot of drama and failed attempts. No one was qualified by a religious system. The one thing they have in common that marked each of them was at some point they stopped listening to fear and took the courage offered to them.

Often, when we are in a difficult moment it feels as though we are destined to stay there. We think, *this is my destiny*. We're right on the edge of what we're dreaming about but paralyzed by not knowing where to start or how to keep moving once we do.

Perhaps the moment that appears marked with the *X* of fear is not only marking your calling but also your chiasm. In fact, the word chiasm is represented by the letter *X* in the Greek alphabet. We all need to see that in the middle of feeling stuck in a Not Yet Zone," God is working on a turnaround we are yet unaware of.

The next time you are at lunch with someone, you're going to sound brilliant. Let your friend know that you are in the middle of a chiasm, and I am pretty sure that anyone overhearing your conversation at the next table is going to say "I'll have what their having". Because who doesn't want a turnaround in their story?

Take a minute to think through where your greatest battle lies right now. All over that battle is fear yelling *stop!* The enemy fights the hardest before the turnaround, but you, brave one, have been wired for leadership to change the world. Behind your greatest battle is your greatest turnaround, and stamped on every one of your failures is its own chiastic structure. The big a-ha moment for me was realizing that if God is inviting me to do something bigger than me, which is all the time these days, He is also offering me the courage to do it. Ultimately, He sees things in me that I don't yet see in myself!

# 14

# Timing is Everything

Have you ever noticed how it's not always convenient to be brave? Sometimes it's downright annoying. Esther's response when asked to be the one to approach the king to save the nation of Israel from a sure annihilation?

*It's been thirty days since I was called to the king.*
Esther 4:11

Umm…can I take a rain check?

It's not convenient right now. Not only have I not seen him for thirty days, but if I approach him without permission, he could kill me. (And you think *you* have problems?) You've got to be kidding me, I don't want to disturb the comfort of this moment. I can't go in; it could mean my life, the end of everything I've grown accustomed to.

I don't know about you, but I have become an expert at wielding a perfect excuse.

If fear doesn't stop us, the inconvenience of its timing will.

Have you ever noticed how we consider time? It seems it's either not moving quickly enough, or it appears to be the most inopportune moment. Like my kids on a road trip, I often wonder if God tires of hearing my constant, "Are we there yet?"

While I could become frustrated at my five-year-old for not sitting still in a waiting room, I find myself squirming just as much with trusting

73

God with His timing. If only I knew how long the middle was going to last, which day I can write the turnaround in my calendar, or how many more miles to the destination, then I could trust Him.

Eternity puts a little perspective on time.

> *In this I rejoice, though now, for a little while if necessary you have been grieved by various trials so that the tested genuineness of your faith—more precious than gold that perishes though it is tested by fire may be found to result in praise and glory and honor at the revelation of Christ.*
> 1 Peter 1:6-7

*Now.*

*For a little while.*

*At the revelation of Christ.*

I love how God sees time.

While we are busy counting down the days until the trial is over, Christ is counting up the days until He is revealed and you see Him. Looking through God's perspective, time becomes a gift. There is no such thing as too late with God…or too inconvenient.

He's never late, as He holds your time in His hands. Your present circumstances may not seem significant to you, but your "behind the scenes" is where the highlight reel of your life is developing. Sometimes God exacts the timing and sometimes He entrusts it.[45]

> *But those who wait on the Lord*
> *Shall renew their strength;*
> *They shall mount up with wings like eagles,*
> *They shall run and not be weary,*
> *They shall walk and not faint.*
> Isaiah 40:31

Waiting is the single most exhausting thing to me. Yet, in this verse, God says that we receive strength and begin to fly when we wait.

Shoot.

How did I miss this?

Not just ordinary strength, either. But walking and running like an Olympic athlete and flying too? Because what pivots exhaustion into strength and flying lessons, is not *what* you're waiting on but *who* you're waiting for. Inherent in the wait is a longing. In other words, if you are longing for relationship with God, and not just waiting for a husband to come along, you will feel fresh wind in that wait. And if that doesn't sling wind under your wings, how about knowing that while you are longing for a deeper relationship with God, He is also longing to be gracious and show you favor[46]—and is watching over His promise to you.[47] His longing and delight for you to experience it is even greater than yours. But not only is He a God of time,

He is a God of perfect timing.

The ability to trust God with the timing and turnaround allows you to adjust the sails of your boat to turn a gale force wind of resistance into a path of purpose. That's being brave in the wait. Whether you feel forced with the timing or entrusted with it, knowing this next key gives you clear vision:

He's never late.

I have tried this before and have become an expert on waiting for the *perfect moment*—you know, when all the pieces fall into place. When it's, you know, perfect.

Somewhere along her journey, Esther began leading herself. She stopped waiting for everything to be *perfect*. She found courage in her voice, took the leadership entrusted to her and resolved to be the change she wanted to see. This young orphaned girl became resolute and chose to see her circumstance differently—and that changed everything.

# 15

# See the Turnaround

*We are what we believe.*

— C. S. Lewis —

Don't you just hate those dressing room mirrors that are slightly warped? You know the ones that make you look a little bigger and more cellulite-y than you'd like to admit? I'm pretty sure I have thought a few times that the manufacturer should have to spend eternity looking at himself in the same mirror that's in my dressing room! I always leave the dressing room feeling that I am bigger than I thought I was. Just a slight change in perspective changes how we see our identity. And so it is with every area of your life.

What you see is who you become. In other words, you have to *see* the leader in you. Your thoughts set your path and guide you to your turn-around. But you can't just stop the thoughts that have kept you feeling like a victim; you have to replace them with thoughts that you are a leader. In fact, the Bible tells us that real transformation happens as a result of a renewed mind.[48] Research shows the average person thinks approximately 50,000 thoughts per day. That's either good or bad news, because every thought moves you either toward your God-given potential or away from it. It instills either fear or courage. Thinking about what you're thinking is leading yourself well. Instead of letting negative self-talk define you, let it become a warning signal and replace it with what God says about you. Whatever you dwell on becomes increasingly prominent in your mind., so focus on your strengths and the good things that are happening right now.[49] (I have included simple daily declarations at the end of each section, for you to begin seeing what God already sees in you).

Esther had to change the way she thought. She went from, "I haven't been called into the king," to rewriting decrees and leading a nation. Her perspective changed, intentionally moving from victim to leader.

The bottom line: God's plan is not threatened by anyone or anything. His purpose *will* come to pass.

Who are you listening to? The limitations of your past or present? Or are you listening to what God says about you?

*So Queen Esther, daughter of Abihail, along with Mordecai the Jew*
*wrote with full authority to confirm this second letter*
*concerning Purim.*
Esther 9:29

Wow; talk about a divine turnaround.

Esther rewrote the law with *full authority*. What was meant to be an epic tragedy became the grandest story of a turnaround in all of Persia. She made the choice to stand up to the enemy of fear. She took the courage handed to her and became the leader God had already called her to be. Her choice to take the courage she was entrusted with turned an entire nation around. She was no longer a victim of her circumstances but had stepped into her full authority.

Esther understood what was being handed to her in the middle of her difficulty. The choice to fall back into the shadows or stand up and lead in the middle of her Not Yet Zone made all the difference. Her consistent *yes* changed how she saw herself. Although nothing around her changed at first, it was Esther's internal turnaround of perspective from victim to leading herself that opened the door to the turnaround for her world. This is *chiasm*: it happens in our hearts in the places we feel stuck, first. And *that* changes everything!

Your story is a profile of courage, and the divine Narrator has already written brave all over it. Time to say yes and use the courage *you've* been entrusted with. I'm convinced there's a world out there that needs your brave.

Like Esther, you have been given authority. In the next section we'll learn about the leadership and authority you've been entrusted with and how to use what's already in your hand. I cannot wait for you to discover it!

## Questions to Ask Yourself:

1. *In what area is fear an indicator to a calling on my life?*
2. *Where do I need to take the courage offered to me?*
3. *In what areas do I need to trust God with the timing, or step into what He's asking now?*

## Declaration:

I declare it's not too late to accomplish everything God has placed in my heart. I have not missed my window of opportunity, but will use my Not Yet Zone as an incubator to empower me. I see the turnaround God has already written into my story, and I take the "brave" being offered to me. I thank God for the unlimited resources He has given me to fulfill His purpose in my life.

## Prayer:

God, I thank you that no matter my current circumstances or how long I've been waiting, you have already written brave into my story. Fear will not hold me back any longer and that I will entrust the timing and turnaround to you. I thank you for the turnaround in my heart by leading myself well. I silence the victim mentality and choose to believe what you say about me. Today I say *yes* to you and that I am yours completely and wholly!

# PART IV

# ENTRUSTED
# WITH
# LEADERSHIP

*You've always had the power my dear, you just had to learn it for yourself.*

— The Wizard of Oz —

# 16

# Take it Back

Awakened at three o'clock in the morning to the sound of car alarms, I jumped from my bed to the window of our Capital Hill home.

There had been a number of cars stolen in our neighborhood over the years (including our daughter's), which was disconcerting to say the least, so I was horrified at that moment to see a couple of young guys sauntering down the road trying to open the doors of every car they passed. But it wasn't until they tried to break into *my* car, setting the car alarm off, that I called the police.

Within seconds three cop cars were cruising down the street with spotlights beaming into the darkest recesses of our neighborhood. As I buried myself back into the warmth of my comforter and pillows, I found myself feeling safe, secure, and confident that nothing would be taken because the "enforcers" were out there protecting us.

Then in the stillness of the night I heard God speak to me.

*Have you been as diligent keeping watch over the promises I have given you that the lies of the enemy have attempted to steal? And not just for you, but for those around you?*

Hmmm…maybe not….

I know enough that when God asks a question it's not because He doesn't know the answer.

How about you, friend?

Can you think of a few things that have been stolen from *you* this week, or this year, or over a lifetime? Were these under the banner of a lie that tells you what you're facing is too big for God to handle?

The mental battles we face daily often steal the joy, peace, purpose, and confidence of unlimited promises God has designed for us. When this happens, our lives become framed as victims of circumstance rather than the leaders God has called us to be.

Listening to the whisper of truth above the din of lies is everything. It's the beginning of taking back what Jesus has already paid for.

What does that look like for you? Here's the simple truth:

What you rise above you have authority over.

Your Not Yet story is about recognizing and using the authority you've been entrusted with. It's an understanding that because Jesus overcame, you can too. And that is leading yourself well.

Discovering your leadership potential in the middle of your Not Yet zone is everything.

It's not about faking perfection, but understanding that every scar and crack is an integral part of your influence as a leader.

It's about taking personal responsibility. Now that you've flipped the switch to expose your fears, realized you've been entrusted with process and the turnaround to live brave, it's time to discover the leader *in* you. Because while you were sleeping, in the "stuck" of comfortably uncomfortable, a thief has had an all-out war on your potential and your story.

The reason why this section is so important is you'll discover how to take back your God given authority, what's rightfully yours with what I call the 10:10 Principle because I've adopted it from John 10:10.

*The thief comes only to steal and kill and destroy; I have come that*
*they may have life, and have it to the full.*
John 10:10

Living a 10:10 life is a daily choice to live abundantly—to take the responsibility of leading yourself by guarding what God has entrusted to you; to believe that what God has to offer you is greater than anything the lies of the enemy attempt to steal, and to understand the shadow of the lie has to eventually succumb to the light of truth.

Lighting a candle in a dark room doesn't extinguish the light; it shatters the darkness.

Truth does that too. It reveals what's hidden in you, exposes the real, magnificent you—who may have been hiding out because of what's being stolen from you.

A number of years ago, the Contemporary Art Museum of Caracas realized that *Odalisque in Red* by Henri Matisse had been stolen several years prior. For more than four years, no one realized the theft had occurred because a counterfeit replaced it in its original frame. Amazingly, looking at the original and the counterfeit side by side exposes the obvious counterfeit; yet it passed even the most discerning eyes—from museum staff to President Hugo Chavez.[50]

I fear an all-out war on your identity and purpose would like to leave you a perfect replica instead of an original, imperfect you. My prayer is you find a way to be yourself.

Who wants a copy when you can have an original? The value of the original of anything is always greater than the counterfeit. Remember, the greatest part of living free is being okay with who you are. The "who you are" is who God uses the most. It's not about a position we're entitled to, but being positioned to use what we've been entrusted with.

So, as I sit here at three thirty in the morning, I've just realized my gym clothes are on inside out, my hair is a hot mess, I have "designer" bags (under my eyes), and I am slightly over-caffeinated. But my heart is full. Thinking of what might happen as you make the words in this book a reality in your life brings tears to my eyes.

I so believe in you, my friend, and so does God. Imagine with me the rippling effect of what will happen in your life when you grasp the truth that you don't have to be stolen from any longer. Not only can you take back your peace, joy, and confidence, but you can also use it to bring hope to someone else. The rippling effect of that gives me goosebumps, (*or it could be the caffeine*) because your deficiency is the perfect starting point for a miracle.

Truett Cathy was one of the top billionaires in the country. He was the founder of Chick-fil-A. He was so tongue-tied he couldn't put three words together. A few weeks after opening his first restaurant, it burned to the ground. Just as the second restaurant was opening, his brother and business partner were killed in a plane crash. What could have been a recipe for failure and limitations became Truett Cathy's greatest motivation.

Cathy once said, "To glorify God by being a faithful steward of all that is entrusted to us and to have a positive of influence on all who come into contact with Chick-fil-A," was one of his greatest values. For Truitt Cathy, chicken was simply a tool to accomplish his real purpose of honoring God and helping people.[51]

Truitt Cathy understood all of the obstacles were part of his story; it was God turning his liabilities into assets. What a profound thought: Chicken was just a tool to accomplish his real purpose—honoring God and *helping people*.

What areas in your life are your "chicken"? That's the stuff God wants to use to accomplish His purpose. God is the author and finisher of my story.[52] What He begins in my life, He finishes. I just have to choose to trust the author.

You see, leading yourself is about what you've chosen to overcome—fear, condemnation, your environment, abuse, illness—and all the stuff you are *still* overcoming.

Have you chosen to forgive the intense pain of offense that once crippled you?

Have you overcome condemnation, abuse, physical handicaps, or an illness?

Maybe your current environment inhibits your progress, but resolutely, step by step, you're overcoming.

Or perhaps your family makes the Kardashian home look tame, but you've decided it's not going to define you.

Queen Esther overcame a victim mentality by not waiting for someone else to speak up and lead the nation. God with her; with every timid step she became bolder as she moved forward. She crushed every lie that told her it wasn't possible. By guarding over what had been entrusted to her, Esther chose to let truth define her story.

It was her story of using what she'd been entrusted with—authority *and* leadership.

Whether you know it or not you have one as well. Believing it *is* possible for God to use you is gold. Believing *you* are possible is everything.

It was for me.

My story was wrought with so much shame and fear from sexual abuse, it was years before I could even talk about it. This was mostly because I didn't understand how God could use me in an imperfect, failed, *not yet* state. Growing up in a church culture that celebrated perfection rather than authenticity kept my gifts hidden and my confidence stifled.

It all changed when I realized God is for me just as I am; that His endless, untiring, relentless love doesn't condemn me, but celebrates who I am right now with every flaw. I don't know why this simplicity is so difficult for us to grasp, but I do know the original conversation with humanity that echoes through the ages is on repeat from the heart of God: *Who told you, you were naked?* My vulnerability and openness to the pain, along with my willingness to forgive and move forward gives me authority to stand and tell you my story, because if I overcame a boatload of failure, so can you. It's all about choosing the voices we listen to. No matter what you have walked through, you must see there is a battle over your life—for your authenticity and your authority. My friend Lisa Bevere says, "The attacks on your life have more to do with who you might be in the future than who you were in the past."[53]

*Blessed is the one who perseveres under trial because, having stood the test, that person will receive the crown of life that the Lord has promised to those who love him.*
James 1:12

The crown gives meaning to the pain, and it gives you the understanding that your *pain* doesn't define you, but what you *overcome* does. Crowns signify authority and leadership. Written into your story of overcoming is what you've been entrusted with. Leadership, authority, and influence, not only for yourself but for others. We know God never wastes a hurt, failure, or difficulty; if we allow Him, He uses it for His purpose.

God will always redeem your story by surrounding you with people who need to hear your past so it doesn't become their future.

No matter how much stress, opposition, and offense you've faced—even when it feels like it's more than you can handle—you can expect double the amount of grace than what you face. God promises that His kindness increases at a faster rate than sin and darkness. His grace is running ahead of whatever it is that is trying to hold you small; in fact, it's already blowing the walls off your place of limitation. He is already ahead of your failed attempts with open arms of grace.

I once attempted to make bread from scratch and I put double the yeast of what the recipe called for then let it set over night. I'm sure you know what happened next. The bread dough expanded to the size of Kansas, overflowing all over the kitchen counter. It even broke the box in which I'd stored it!

> But where sin increased, [God's remarkable, gracious gift of] grace
> [His unmerited favor] has surpassed it and increased all the more.
> Romans 5:20 (AMP)

If you let Him, God will take the weakest part of your life and make it the strongest part of your faith. He is more determined that the 10:10 Principle work in your life than you could ever imagine. The Bible says that the truth will set us free.[54] Actually, it's the truth we *know* that sets us free, which requires some intentionality on our part!

Let's take a moment to discover the source of the authority you've been entrusted with and how to live in the freedom of that truth.

# 17

# Consider the Source of the Trust Fund

The first part of the process of using the authority you've been entrusted with is understanding the source of the trust fund. If we don't recognize the value of the inheritance that has been left to us through the sacrifice of Christ and His word, we will miss the investment of the trust, and quite possibly live like a trust fund baby without a purpose. The light on my desk only sheds the light I need on my notes when I have it plugged into the power source. In the same way, unless you know the accuracy of the source and what you actually have been entrusted with, it's difficult to stand with authority. You will swim in a sea of "I hope I can" and lose sight of the "I know I can" life.

From the beginning, God wanted us to consider *Him* as the source of everything. He spoke the world into existence. Everything we see in our world began as a word from God. Everything from the lush landscape around us to the number of thoughts we have each day and the hairs on our head is a detail He is concerned with. If you remove a plant from the source, it dies; if you remove a fish from its source it dies; if you take humanity from God you've robbed Him of His life source and purpose.

*I ask—ask the God of our Master, Jesus Christ, the God of glory—to make you intelligent and discerning in knowing him personally,*

*your eyes focused and clear, so that you can see exactly what it is he
is calling you to do, grasp the immensity of this glorious way of life
he has for his followers, oh, the utter extravagance of his work in us
who trust him—endless energy, boundless strength!*
Ephesians 1:18-19 (MSG)

Paul said he prayed for the church at Ephesus, that they would be intelligent and discerning in knowing God personally. He prayed that their eyes were clear and focused so they could see and *grasp the immensity* of what God was calling them to do.

The size of your God should determine the size of your dream.

Not the size of your education, family, experiences, or even your gifts—because while they all add to what you've been given, they will limit where you go if you only rely on them and don't consider the magnitude of *the* source.

If you had access to the full resources of anything you wanted from the corner store, that would be amazing, right? You could grab the milk, butter, or even the chocolate you always seem to need. But how much different would it be if Warren Buffet was your source? That would change *everything.* You wouldn't just have access to the milk, butter, or chocolate at the corner store; you'd have access to the cow, the farm, *and* the Godiva factory. Well you get it; you'd have unlimited resource and supply (which would be pure heaven and hell for me, as I would then need access to the stretchy pants factory to fit into the sudden growth of my behind).

Perhaps we have missed the magnitude of what we've been entrusted with because we haven't looked in the right place for it. To find *your* unique purpose, you must begin by going back to the main source—God.

*It's in Christ that we find out who we are and what we are living
for. Long before we first heard of Christ and got our hopes up, He
had His eye on us, had designs for our glorious living, part of the
overall purpose he is working out in everything and everyone."*
Ephesians 1:11-12 (MSG)

In fact, the only accurate way to understand ourselves is by what God is and by what God does for us.[55] When we look to the true source of potential, we discover that He promises to fulfill His purpose in us. Everyone is born with a wealth of potential; the trust that's been given to you is unlimited; the resources are beyond your current viewpoint.

You are a trust fund baby *with* purpose.

What have you been entrusted with to overcome? What gifts, strengths, or talents do you possess? What has the journey deposited in you as a "trust" from the "Funder" in heaven? Every single experience you have walked through is a deposit into the trust fund that Jesus set up for you.

That creative gift, the touch you add to everything? You've been entrusted with that. That administrative gift and the desire to put all of life in a spreadsheet? Yep, you've been entrusted with it. Your ability to see a problem and the solution? That's a gift. You keep a cool head and remain calm in a storm? Or you're the one who takes charge and leads the parade? All of it—a gift. Until we can see our experiences as gifts we've been entrusted with, we won't realize the authority we've been given.

After several years of homeschooling our youngest child, we enrolled him in a private middle school. Readjusting was a little difficult for Evan, as he navigated the classroom setting. He was like a kid in a candy store; he loved having constant interaction with friends—so much that he had a problem with continuous talking. He talked so much that I began receiving weekly phone calls from his teacher that turned into regular meetings with his principal. I was told he wouldn't listen and talked non-stop. The more this continued, the more we began to question the decision to send him back to a traditional school, and also began to question his future.

Gosh, if he had a hard time listening to his teacher and was always in time out, maybe he really had a problem with authority. My mind easily dove into a downward spiral: if he has a problem with authority now, then he always will. Before I knew it, in my head I was visiting him in prison because he just couldn't listen. Picturing him in an orange jumpsuit was just too overwhelming! I was heartbroken to think our son, who we believed had a bright future, could someday end up in prison.

Ridiculous, right?

But one day a friend of mine interrupted this craziness in my head and gave me a fresh take (which God *knew* I needed). As I told her the story and my greatest fears, she reassured me what was happening was Evan's *gift* of communication was actually bursting at the seams. His gift of gab wasn't a weakness, but a grace on his life he had been entrusted with. As his parents, we were to speak into that gift, and then teach him how to direct it, submit it, and use it for good.

A gift of communication. Wow. That was a game changer.

Daily, Dennis and I began to declare the grace we saw on Evan's life. We spoke over him, that he was *gifted* with communication, a leader *submitted* to authority, that he was the answer—not the problem, that he had the mind of Christ...and on it went. We wanted that imbedded into his life and not the echo of feeling like he didn't fit.

Each of us is brilliantly and uniquely designed and entrusted with *something*.

Including you, my friend.

You may be thinking at this point, "Awesome, but I'm not sure what I have is significant. When God was passing out the gifts and talents He was scraping the bottom of the barrel when he came to me." Or, like Evan, you may only see the struggle in the shadow of what God has placed in you.

You may feel that God can't use you, that you're handicapped in some way. "Once I get through this season, then I'll be ready," you think. "Let me just get myself together."

But when I read about the legends in the Bible, I realize none of them felt "ready" when God called on them. They just said yes and invited God into their handicap. He used all kinds of people—kings, slaves, prostitutes, liars, deceivers, fakers, and even a donkey. It's crazy to think that nineteen books of the Bible were written by murderers! Not one of them was qualified by today's religious standards. In fact, if you and I had to pick someone for the job, we certainly wouldn't have picked any of them.

Which is exactly why we don't pick ourselves! We have become so familiar with the personal perception of inadequacies and limitations we think they're what we were destined to. We've become used to living small in a confined place, our thoughts imprisoning us as we mentally don our "orange jumpsuits".

It's time to give power to the right stuff. It's time to move into the wide open spaces of *endless possibilities* God has designed for you! You, friend, were born *by* His purpose and *for* His purpose.

# 18

# Consider the Value of the Trust Fund

Perhaps one of the reasons you haven't seen it is because the battle waged over you is attempting to obscure your view. You've heard your deficiencies screaming at you, not realizing it's the starting point of a God miracle.

*Command those who are rich in this present world not to be arrogant nor to put their hope in wealth, which is so uncertain, but to put their hope in God, who richly provides us with everything for our enjoyment. Command them to do good, to be rich in good deeds, and to be generous and willing to share. In this way they will lay up treasure for themselves as a firm foundation for the coming age, so that they may take hold of the life that is truly life. Timothy, guard what has been entrusted to your care.*
1 Timothy 6:17-20 (NIV)

You only guard things that have great value. Everything from jewelry stores to top level government security have layers of protection because of their value. If God is asking me to guard over what He has entrusted to me, then it must mean *He* places great value on it. And if we have to guard it, that means it has the potential to be stolen! If we don't realize this, we can go years without realizing it was ours from the start.

Recognizing the thing that makes you valuable also makes you vulnerable. We decide what we are vulnerable to, the lies or the access to what's been given to us. If you are struggling right now, it is a sure sign of the value of the good deposit in you.

One of my favorite stories is a parable of a wealthy landowner and how[56] he delegates the management of his wealth to his servants, much as investors in today's markets do. He gives five talents (a large unit of money) to one, two talents to another, and one talent to a third. Two of the servants earn a hundred percent return by trading with the funds, but the third servant hides his talent in the ground, earning nothing. The profound significance of the parable extends far beyond finances and wealth and is a clear reminder that God has entrusted each of us with a variety of gifts and talents He wants to use.

I find it fascinating that the wealthy landowner (re: God) was acutely aware of what was happening to the wealth he had given to his servants. The inference is he *wants* to see what he entrusts to them *grow*. He actually celebrated the growth by giving more to the ones who doubled what they were given. While each was given a different amount—according to their ability—it was actually using the investment that grew the ability and the impact of their influence. The servant with the one talent wasn't condemned for not making it a five-talent gift but for hiding what he had been given. It wasn't acceptable to merely hide or ignore what was entrusted by the Master.

It's such a beautiful picture that we are to invest our lives and not allow fear to keep what God makes possible hidden on a shelf.

As I look back over my life, I wish I had recognized earlier on that God is the source; I wish I'd realized He was *for me*, that He is more about me trying even with failed attempts rather than sitting and hiding what He has paid a price for me to have. I wouldn't have wasted so many years digging ditches to hide what He has entrusted in me to invest in others.

Perhaps you've been praying for favor and increase and God is saying, "I've already placed in you what you need to see that happen; stop waiting and hiding it and start using what's in your hand."

Recognize your ability.

All three servants in the parable had been gifted, just not equally. The landowner gave his servants gifts according to their abilities. He'd previously assessed what they could handle. You can grow that ability, that talent, that gift by taking action: going to school, training under a mentor, reading books—there is no end to the resources available to help you grow your abilities.

If you invest the ability that's been invested in you, it multiplies.

All three servants were given two things: talent and an opportunity. The opportunity is often hidden. If we are not careful we will be distracted by the busyness and inequity of life (he has more than me!). Sometimes what illuminates the gift or talent is the hard stuff you walk through.

So while you are in the middle of your turnaround, in the Not Yet Zone, and you keep thinking, *get me outta here! Then I will invest my talents, my goods, and my efforts,* God is saying right there in that place there is opportunity.

In the opposition is the opportunity.

The servant who was given one talent let the opposition and fear shut him down; therefore, even the little bit he had was taken away; he missed the opportunity. When asked why he hid the money he said, he perceived the master too demanding.

Think about it; all the servants were all exposed to the same information; the others weren't privy to anything additional. How you process your situation and how you view God determines your outcome, and it's your processing that either builds or hinders your potential. Choosing to change your perspective of God from an angry tyrant to a loving, grace filled rewarder opens the door to *endless possibilities.*[57]

Whether you are a one, two, or five talent person, you have something to give! It's your story of overcoming, your story of faithfully staying the path. You keep looking for a fully formed oak tree, but God says, *I've given you an acorn; use what's in your hand and watch what grows out of that.* God has given you the talent, ability, and opportunity, you just need to recognize it in a seed form in the middle of the opposition.

It's Sunday morning and I sit in church amazed at the grace of God. Hunter and Joy are on our pastoral team at one of our Capital City Church campuses. As they sit in the front row with their three beautiful little girls, it's still hard to believe what they walked through just a few months prior.

They had been on a family vacation at Hunter's parents' home when their then two-year-old, Harper, fell into the swimming pool and was without oxygen for eighteen minutes. In spite of security fences and cameras and stellar parenting, Hunter and Joy faced every parent's worst nightmare. Hunter discovered Harper unconscious floating lifelessly in the deep end of the pool.

With the help of the EMTs who were only minutes away, they finally got a pulse and Harper began breathing again. Once in the hospital, though, they received the dismal report that if Harper did live, she would most likely have no brain function after being without oxygen for eighteen minutes. But in the darkest place they found opportunity. Joy realized in the hospital that *all* of the scripture she had been studying in the Bible just a few weeks prior in her daily devotional time would become the declarations they would make over Harper's healing. She and Hunter posted these scriptures, as well as others, all over Harper's hospital room and on social media.

What became a global ground swell of prayer, known as #harpersmiracle, turned into a story of how God used a devastating experience of great opposition and turned it into an opportunity that touched hundreds of lives far from God. The acorn of potential in Joy and Hunter grew into a mighty oak of faith to see a death-to-life picture of what God can do. Faithfully stewarding the little they'd been given and partnering with what they believed God wanted to do, they were firsthand witnesses to the power of God.

Harper remained in the hospital for just under two weeks; the medical experts agreed this was a legitimate miracle as the little girl who was not expected to live is now a fully functioning three-year-old.

Maybe you're not facing a life or death experience right now. Maybe you just need a little faith to believe God can use you where you are right now. Remember, the simplicity of using what you have to serve someone else always opens you up to witness a miracle. The servants at the first wedding Jesus attended were the ones to experience the miracle firsthand when what they were pouring from vats turned from water to the finest wine.

As unqualified as you may feel know that the purpose you were created for is always going to be bigger than you; you just have to start somewhere.

If you use the little that's in your hand, watch how God multiplies it. The servant with five talents thought, *how can I use my experience, failures, my opposition, my season, and my grace to make it* more. The servant with two talents thought, *I believe I can turn this into double what I was handed.*

Entrusted thinking is always, *how can I multiply?*

Always thinking about how to grow, steward, and increase what has been given. All three had abilities and were exposed to opportunity, but their perspective changed everything.

Here's some encouragement for you. If you have a level-two talent, work the two. Stop comparing your two talents to someone else's five talents and open your eyes to see where you can invest.

When the servants with two and five talents returned with what they had invested and increased, their master told them they would be given even more: more influence and more authority.

What they overcame they now had authority over.

If you use what's been given to you, you're leading yourself well—and that means your capacity, confidence, and authority increases! When you give what you have, it only increases you.

I met her when she was a freshman at George Washington University. New to the city, she quickly became one of our favorites as we adopted her into our family; her quick wit and sense of humor were always a delight to be around. But we saw something in Hannah she didn't yet see. Her creativity, while still in acorn form, had the ability to grow and touch many. And Hannah could sing. Oh, could she sing! She'd open her mouth and heaven would fill the room. But Hannah was weighted down with so much fear that she would often get sick to her stomach before going on stage to lead worship in our services. You would never know when she started singing what might have happened just fifteen minutes prior!

As Hannah continued to push past her fear, her confidence and authority grew, and that timid girl who first stepped onto the stage is long gone. Every step, often a scared *yes* into what she'd been entrusted with began to enlarge her world. Hannah says, "in that stretch is where I met Jesus and I discovered God as a source I wouldn't have seen if I didn't step out. If you just use what's in your hand, though seemingly insignificant, God will always increase it." Not only does Hannah use her story to coach others who are paralyzed with fear, she is an avid blogger and has started a successful company, Piccadilly Creative, on the side of her day job. If Hannah had stayed hidden in opposition, she would have never discovered the gifts that have blossomed in her life.

Reappraise the value of the calling of Christ on your life. If you're struggling with following through on an opportunity, reappraise. If you're struggling with your kids, reappraise. Your struggle is not a sign that you're useless or ungifted, it's a sign of your value. The battle is over your potential and your authority. It's time to stop basing your authority on the circumstances surrounding your life right now. Use what's in your hand.

It was a glorious morning. I awoke early to watch the sunrise on the beach and spend some much needed time reading and praying. As I sat there, I drank my morning supply of caffeine and reflected on how happy I was to be on a Caribbean beach celebrating thirty-five years of wedded bliss with my husband. Actually to be honest, I was just so incredibly grateful we'd won that battle over the early years to finally *be* on the "wedded bliss" side our marriage. As I took in the view, I spotted a few hotel employees walking back and forth in front of me, raking the sand. At first I didn't notice them, but the more they blocked my view, the more irritated I became. Seriously? Didn't they know I was the customer who had paid to be there and was entitled to this spot and this view?

I'd lost most all of the quiet and peace I'd garnered previously when I heard God speak to me. *Stop feeling entitled to what you think is yours and realize what you've been entrusted in this moment.*

Right. What could I possible have to offer in this moment?

As my frustration began to fade, I began to *really* see the workers in front of me. Compassion for them began to well up as I considered what their lives might be like; their jobs involved long, thankless days and I imagined they didn't have a lot to show for it at home. My entitlement quickly melted into the humility of what I had been entrusted with at a great cost. I realized what I had been entrusted with at that moment was prayer; that the power of me standing in the gap for these two guys might very well change their lives.

I jumped up from my seat and went to them to tell them how thankful I was and how much I appreciated their work. Then I asked how I could pray for them. It was a sweet moment I would have completely missed as they opened up their life to me. Their whole countenance was different and so was mine just by taking two minutes to change my perspective.

We are always entrusted with something for the moment we are in, even it if is simply just prayer or a simple word of encouragement. How often in the craziness of my life do I not *really* see the people right in front of me? I ask God to use me, then walk right past fifteen people who irritate me because in the moment they are *in my way*!

What's the acorn in your hand, my friend? Still not sure? Never think it's too late or what you have to offer is insignificant. There will always be someone who needs what you have to offer.

Always. Discover the treasure *in you*.

# 19

# Consider what's in your Hand

This whole process is all about moving from simply surviving to living a life of significance, using the authority you've gained from each step of your journey, and discovering the leadership you've been entrusted with to propel you forward. No longer are your circumstances or your past leading you. You are following Christ and leading yourself, defined by purpose and the unlimited cache of potential.

The fun in the journey is discovering the treasure of what God made possible in *you*.

Your *Gloria*.

In the Not Yet Zone, the time is now to use what you have. Saying yes to what's in front of you, and getting a move on it, friend.

> So here's what I want you to do, God helping you: Take your everyday, ordinary life – your sleeping, eating, going – to – work, and place it before God as an offering. Embracing what God does for you is the best thing you can do for him…readily recognize what He wants from you, and quickly respond to it. God brings the best out of you, develops well-formed maturity in you.
> Romans 12:1-2 MSG

Now that you understand the source of what you've been entrusted with, the value of those gifts, let's begin to map out how to discover them. Here are five things to consider while trying to discover what is in your hand:

- *What are my strengths? What am I gifted to do?*
- *What's in my heart? What am I naturally passionate about and love to do?*
- *What are my natural abilities? (Maybe your good with numbers, you like kids or sports, or you collect cats?)*
- *What is my personality? (Routine? Variety?)*
- *What are my experiences? (Vocational, family, educational, spiritual...)*

So where do you start?

You start by using whatever your current occupation is, pharmacist, lawyer, teacher, mother, nanny, retiree, etc. and ask yourself this question every day:

*How can I use _____ in service to something bigger and greater than my paycheck or myself?*

I guarantee your whole life will shift when you go to work or become involved with a new project and you begin to daily ask yourself this question. You'll find this simple question opens your eyes to see incredible opportunity right where you are. The turnaround starts by recognizing it *before* you feel like you're ready, before the breakthrough, when you simply think on God's purposes for your life in that very moment.

You could possibly be the answer to someone else finding their significance in the middle of their Not Yet story. There is no greater feeling of satisfaction and significance than when you use the unique experience, strengths, passions and personality you've been entrusted with to encouage someone else. Every time you say yes to an opportunity to be used by God, it increases your leadership capacity and enlarges your world.

*The goal of life is to not have our lives mean something to ourselves; the goal in life is to have our lives mean something to others.*[58]

— Simon Sinek —

We are all affected by turnaround stories; we are all touched when someone overcomes something and then uses that experience to impact someone else.

God wired us that way. Maybe you haven't realized the capital you've gained yet, but that you keep going, keep showing up, and are determined to move forward in life keeps adding to your trust fund. And daily, God is setting you up to impact someone's world, be it your co-worker, that single mom whose kids are out of control and is struggling to pay her rent, that neighbor who is difficult to talk to, your negative coworker, your kids and husband.

Yeah.

Often those are God set-ups, because you have been entrusted with a story of overcoming that will impact someone else's journey.

*I press on so that I may lay hold of that for which also I was laid hold of by Christ Jesus…. forgetting what is behind and reaching towards the prize of the high calling of Christ.*
Philippians 3:12-14

When I stand before God one day, I hope I can say "I pressed through the fear, failure, imperfections and used everything you gave me."

So I've made it my daily practice to reach for the calling to lead, to stretch for the light switch and no longer soothe my fears but take the authority and the brave entrusted to me to expose the lies. Intentional on living a life of significance that is making an impact on the world around me right in the middle of my Not Yet Zone.

You can do this too!

Fight for it. Take it and go change the world with what's in your hand.

Lead yourself well.

You've got this friend; I believe in you, and am cheering *you* on.

Perhaps at the end of time, your Creator will tell the story of *your* life. It'll probably sound something like this:

"Once upon a time, in the days of the great King Jesus of the vast empire of heaven and earth, there was someone who thought they were forgotten; their name was_____ (your name) and this is the story of how they discovered God's love and favor. With noble acts, costly grace, and great authority they fought their battles. This is the story of how they rose up and what they overcame, story after story of a Hero's journey, how *their* story collided with *His* story, and how their bold declarations gave liberty to countless captives."

With drama and emotion, the King will tell your story of how amidst unsurmountable obstacles, you didn't stop. Failed attempts only garnered strength and taught you how to win in the Not Yet Zone; the echo of your story resounding for generations as you discovered you had come to the kingdom for such a time as this.[59]

## Questions to Ask Yourself:

1. *What lies have I been listening to that have stolen my potential?*
2. *What's in my hand? Take some time to answer the questions on page 102.*
3. *Discover more about the way you are wired by taking this free online personality test. Have fun while doing it! https://www.16per-sonalities.com/*
4. *Where can I start using my story, gifts, and passion to bring strength to someone else?*

## Declaration:

I will lead myself and be the change I want to see in the world. I will use the gifts God has entrusted to me from what I have overcome with authority. I believe He is able to do exceedingly abundantly above what I ask or think according the power that works within me. I won't just look for a solution; I will *be* the solution by using my gifts to impact others everywhere I go. I believe I am a world changer on the planet for such a time as this.

**Prayer:**

God, in the name of Jesus I thank you for entrusting me with gift s, strengths, and more than I can even fathom. I choose to lead myself well by following you and listening to your direction and guidance. Set me up daily to use what you've put in my hand to help someone else today. I declare I have an unlimited source of supply. I choose to develop my gift s, abilities, and talents to multiply what you have given me for your glory. Use me to be the change in my world!

Did you enjoy The Power of Not Yet? Please consider leaving your review of the book at www.Amazon.com

# Prayer of Invitation

Knowing God loves you with an extravagant, unlimited love and that His desire for relationship with you is everything. Nothing you have done can keep Him from loving you and nothing you can do can make Him love you any more than He already does. He is love—the most exquisite picture of what it means to be loved without any conditions. He desires you and He wants a relationship with you. In Romans 10:9,10 the bibile says "If you declare with your mouth, "Jesus is Lord" and believe in your heart that God raised him from the dead, you will be saved.

Relationship with God is not about a moral code or a religious system. It is simply saying yes to an invitation he gave 2000 years ago on the cross by praying this prayer:

*Lord Jesus I repent of my sin, come into my heart, wash me clean, I believe in you. I make you my Lord and Saviour, give me a fresh start and a hope and future with you.*

If you have prayed this prayer today, please email me at donnapisani77@gmail.com so I can send you some resources to help you continue to grow in your relationship with Jesus.

# How to Lead Yourself Well:

1.  Spend time daily in the Word. What God says trumps the lies of your situation.
    *   Use the YouVersion Bible app www.youversion.com
        *   Read the daily verse, or start a Bible reading plan; there are hundreds to choose from on the app.
        *   Find a favorite chair or space that feels comfortable. Commit to read for fifteen minutes every morning, first thing.
        *   Read, pray, and write down what you hear God speaking to you from that verse in a journal every day.
2.  Find a mentor; don't wait for one to find you!
    *   Virtual mentors—Listen regularly to their podcasts; read their blogs and books.
    *   In person—find someone you admire who is further along on the journey than you and ask their for fifteen minutes of their time. Come ready with a few questions you want answers to. Be prepared and value their time.
    *   Serve a mentor. Find someone you respect who you can serve: watch their kids; help with the yard work or volunteer at their office. Find out where help is needed and just serve without expectation. You'll find what you glean from those times is often more than what you can in an hour conversation.
3.  Attend and serve in your local church regularly.
    *   What you gain from regular commitment to a community of faith is priceless.
    *   Be a regular attender; the Bible says "those planted in the house of God will flourish."[60]
    *   Get involved by serving in some capacity, using your story and gifts to help others!
    *   God asks us to do life in community, which is often messy as there are no perfect churches; but it will build your character and the life stories of turnarounds you encounter will build your faith.

# Additional Resources:

Gifts Finder Test: Discover More about how God has Uniquely Wired You
www.16personalities.com

One Thousand Gifts by Ann Voscamp

The Sisterhood by Bobbie Houston

Strengths Based Leadership: Great Leaders, Teams, and Why People Follow

Next Generation Leader by Andy Stanley

Unashamed by Christine Caine

Find your Brave by Holly Wagner

See Life Differently by Joel Holm

Girls with Swords by Lisa Bevere

Daring Greatly by Brene Brown

Live, Love Lead by Brian Houston

David and Goliath by Malcolm Gladwell

Start with Why by Simon Sinek

The 4:8 Prinicple by Tommy Newberry

The Prodigal God by Timothy Keller

The Circle Maker by Mark Batterson

# About the Author

Donna Pisani and her husband Dennis are the pastors of Capital City Church (www.capcitychurch.com) in Washington, DC, where she is the founder of Beautiful You (bymovement.com) and co-founder of The Rising DC (therisingdc.com) . She's a dreamer, loves adventure and lives for date night with Dennis, family time with her four kids, and a daily supply of coffee and chocolate. Her greatest passion is to see people empowered to live a life of endless possibilities, connecting with their unique, God given purpose and living fully in their leadership gift.

You can read more from Donna Pisani and stay connected at www.donnapisani.org

# Bibliography

1   Anders, Mae, 30 *Days to Understanding the Bible*, Nashville, TN, Thomas Nelson Publishers 2004, Printed. Page 65

2   http://www.goodreads.com/quotes/445606-being-the-richest-man-in-the-cemetery-doesn-t-matter-to

3   https://www.competitivedge.com/quote-2166

4   http://variety.com/2014/biz/news/disney-brands-generate-record-40-9-billion-from-licensed-merchandise-in-2013-1201221813/

5   http://www.dailymail.co.uk/tvshowbiz/article-2236946/The-Beatles-audition-tape-rejected-discovered-50-years.html

6   https://www.psychologytoday.com/blog/high-octane-women/201210/13-quotes-help-you-face-your-fears

7   http://www.biography.com/people/albert-einstein-9285408

8   http://jackcanfield.com/author/jackcanfield/

9   http://news.harvard.edu/gazette/story/2008/06/text-of-j-k-rowling-speech/

10   Jeremiah 1:5 NLT

11   Luke 12:7

12   1 Peter 5:8

13   http://blogs.psychcentral.com/relationships-balance/2013/03/16/the-grass-is-greener-syndrome/

[14] Monk Kidd, Sue, The Invention of Wings, New York, NY, Penguin Books, 2014. Pg 81. Print.

[15] Genesis 3:1-11

[16] http://www.truenorthquest.com/rudyard-kipling/

[17] Proverbs 18:21 KJV

[18] 2 Timothy 3:16

[19] 1 John 1:8

[20] 2 Corinthians 3:5

[21] Verghese, Abraham, Cutting for Stone, New York, NY: Vintage Books, 2010. Print. Pg 7

[22] http://www.businessinsider.com/a-neuroscience-researcher-reveals-4-rituals-that-will-make-you-a-happier-person-2015-

[23] Romans 5:1-2 MSG

[24] https://www.ted.com/talks/carol_dweck_the_power_of_believing_that_you_can_improve?language=en

[25] Genesis 29,31

[26] http://www.philvaz.com/apologetics/LeonardoLastSupper.htm

[27] Brown, Brene, Daring Greatly, New York, NY: Avery Publications, 2012. Printed. Pages 21-111

[28] Brown, Brene, Daring Greatly, New York, NY, Avery Publications, 2012. Printed. Pages 21-111

[29] Romans 5:5 MSG

[30] Philippians 4:19

[31] Brown, Brene, Daring Greatly, New York, New York, Avery Publishing. Print. Pages 21-111

[32] http://www.goodreads.com/quotes/34941

[33] 1 John 4:18

34 Brown, Brene, *The Gifts of Imperfection*, Hazelden Publishing, Center City, MN: Print.

35 Psalm 138:8 NKJV

36 *Brown, Brene, The Gifts of Imperfection*, Hazelden Publishing, Center City, MN: Print. Page 50

37 http://www.businessinsider.com/a-neuroscience-researcher-reveals-4-rituals-that-will-make-you-a-happier-person-2015-9

38 Manning, Brennan, Colorado Springs, CO, Navpress, Abbas Child: *The Cry of the Heart for Intimate Belonging*. 2015 Print.

39 Moore, Beth, Esther It's Tough Being a Woman, Nashville TN Lifeway, 2008 Print.

40 Anders, Max, 30 Days to Understanding the Bible, Nashville TN, Thomas Nelson Publishing.1988. Print. Pg 11

41 https://en.wikiquote.org/wiki/Rosa_Parks

42 https://en.wikiquote.org/wiki/Amelia_Earhart

43 Sherrill, John and Elizabeth, *The Hiding Place*, Old Tappan, NJ: Fleming Revell Publishing, 1979. Print.

44 http://www.usatoday.com/story/news/nation-now/2013/12/05/nelson-mandela-quotes/3775255/

45 Moore, Beth, Children of the Day, Nashville, TN Lifeway Publishers pg 163

46 Isaiah 30:18

47 Jeremiah 1:2

48 Romans 12:2

49 Newberry, Tommy, The 4:8 Principle, Carol Stream, IL: Tyndale House Publishers. Print. Pg 11

50 http://www.nytimes.com/2012/07/20/world/americas/stolen-matisse-odalisque-in-red-pants-surfaces.html

51 https://en.wikipedia.org/wiki/Chick-fil-A

52 Hebrews 12:2 NKJV

53 Bevere, Lisa, *Girls with Swords*, Danvers, MA: Crown Publishing, 2014 Print.

54 John 8:32

55 Psalm 138:8

56 Matthew 25:14-29

57 Romans 8:37,39
John 3:16
Ephesians 2:4,5
Romans 5:8
Zephaniah 3:17
Psalm 86:15

58 https://www.ted.com/talks/simon_sinek_why_good_leaders_make_ you_feel_safe/transcript?language=en

59 Adapted from Moore, Beth, Esther It's Tough Being a Woman, Nashville TN Lifeway, 2008 Print.

60 Psalm 92:13

Made in the USA
Columbia, SC
12 September 2018